Creating a Scottish Parliament

Creating a Scottish Parliament
Alan Balfour

With a foreword by Rt. Hon. George Reid, Presiding Officer of the Scottish Parliament, and an introduction by Professor David McCrone, Professor of Sociology, and Director, Institute of Governance, University of Edinburgh.

Preface

This book was conceived by the architects Michael Duncan and John Richards. It was they who invited me to shape and develop the essays. They had worked together in the past at Robert Matthew Johnson Marshall and Partners, the antecedent to RMJM, the Scottish side of the architectural partnership. While Enric Miralles was alive Michael Duncan was one of his most creative collaborators and John Richards, Duncan's senior colleague, was a passionate defender of the project (sadly he died in 2003 before he could see the completed building). In the face of criticism, particularly in the press, they felt the need for a document that would make this complex work of public art both accessible and enjoyable to the broad audience for whom it was created. It was also Michael who invited David McCrone to join me in the task; this perceptive and witty scholar of devolution is the most able to present the political context for which the architecture is both symbol and instrument.

I was able to visit the project every three months while under construction and saw and felt it coming to existence. I met and discussed the work with many who contributed to its final form, from the carpenters to the project managers, but my understanding was particularly enhanced in discussion with several people, principal among them Dr John Gibbons, chief architect of the Scottish Office Construction Group, the team entrusted with commissioning and producing the building. Dr Gibbons organised the competition and sat at the centre of all the complex pressures that brought programme and architecture together. John R. Hume, historian of Scottish industry and archaeology, and formerly Chief Inspector of Historic Buildings for Historic Scotland, was not only the authority on the site chosen for the parliament, but both he and David McCrone were patient and perceptive critics of my prose and my knowledge of Scotland.

Michael Duncan was my most persistent critic, but only with the unflagging support of his assistant Elaine Lamont was the exchange maintained between New York and Edinburgh. I am particularly pleased that the book has been designed by Lucy Richards, the daughter of John Richards. I thank them all.

But none of this work would have been possible without access to the extraordinary conceptual material – drawings, sketches, models and notes with which Miralles captured his thoughts as he worked. For that and for her help in the design I am most grateful to architect Benedetta Tagliabue, the wife of Enric Miralles who continued to lead his office after his death.

Alan Balfour
New York, September 2004

Foreword
Rt. Hon. George Reid

At the Opening of Holyrood in October 2004, the Queen quoted Winston Churchill on rebuilding Westminster after the Second World War. 'We shape our buildings,' he said, 'and then they shape us.'

Creating a Scottish Parliament tells the story of how the new Scottish Parliament was shaped. David McCrone and Alan Balfour provide unique insights into the historical, architectural, environmental and governance issues, which inspired the construction of our new home at the bottom end of Edinburgh's Canongate.

The Parliament, as the Queen noted, undoubtedly had a 'difficult and controversial birth'. That perhaps was inevitable, given Enric Miralles' driving vision of a parliamentary campus which would, on a World Heritage site, link the land of Scotland with its people. A place where our thousand years of history in the Royal Mile would fuse with the primeval hills and greenery of Holyrood Park.

A place which would mould Scotland's future.

In 1945, Winston Churchill went back to the past. He wanted a legislature rebuilt in the great traditions of nineteenth-century representative democracy: a small, tightly-packed Chamber, with Government and Opposition facing each other a confrontational two swords' lengths apart.

In 1998, Donald Dewar wanted a legislature appropriate to the twenty-first century. A building which reflected the participative work of the Scottish Constitutional Convention, and paid more than a passing nod to the older traditions, north of the Border, of the sovereignty of the people.

Miralles' parliament is therefore neither grand nor patrician. For those of us who work there, it feels more like a village – a natural continuation of the Royal Mile, with its marketplace in the Garden Lobby, and its nooks and crannies reflecting the vennels and closes of the Old Town of Edinburgh and the barrios of Barcelona.

It is undoubtedly a work of art. The paeans of praise from architectural critics around the world – 'A thrilling masterpiece', 'Britain's most important new building', 'A construction to rival the Forth Rail Bridge' – are testimony to that.

It is now up to its occupants to turn that work of art into a working parliament.

Of course, it was never going to be possible to create a new political culture in Scotland overnight. After three hundred years of centralised decision-making down south, the pull towards the Westminster way of doing things remains strong. A whole new generation of legislators at Holyrood will take a little time to learn their trade.

But if we listen to the building, it will help us. If we converse with the people in the Canongate – the rich and the poor crammed into a small urban space, as always in Edinburgh's history, and the hundreds of thousands of visitors expected each year – they will remind us of why we are here. If we think back on who has been here before, they will spur us on.

Virtually everyone who was anyone in Scotland's story has walked the streets outside Holyrood: the early Scots monarchs, Mary Queen of Scots, Bonnie Prince Charlie, Robert Burns and Walter Scott – and, most importantly, the philosophers, economists and practical men of science who through the Scottish Enlightenment did much to invent the modern world.

In Queensberry House, where the Presiding Officer now works, the Duke of that name plotted the end of the Old Scots Parliament. Our small country then found itself in a common market with a much more powerful neighbour. David Hume, Thomas Reid, Adam Smith (buried, incidentally, just across the road in the Canongate Kirkyard) and the other luminaries of the Englightenment were in consequence forced to think hard about governance and enterprise in a new world.

Scotland today faces similar challenges. How, in particular, do we create a sustainable society, comfortable with itself at home, in Britain and in Europe, and competent at competing in the global marketplace? How, in an age where the state shares power at sub-state and supra-state levels, does Scotland fit? And how, at a time of wide public disengagement from the political process, does the citizen make his or her voice heard?

Miralles has done much to break down the monolithic nature of decision-making. He has created a layered and shared space which invites the people in. He has designed a focal point of national life, as he said in his initial submission, not for sterile confrontation but for shared conversation.

We must keep the conversation going with the citizens of Scotland. The Parliament belongs to them, not the politicians. Our land and our history have shaped us as an egalitarian society, reflected in our founding principles of Accessibility, Accountability, Equality of Opportunities and the sharing of power between our government, parliament and people. These are our real foundation stones.

So here, in the Canongate, is a place which says to all – our wealth creators, thinkers, civic and voluntary Scotland, the whole community of the realm – 'Come on in'.

A place where now, with devolution, if we Scots make mistakes they will be our mistakes, and we can no longer blame anyone else.

A place where we know our enemy. And have the wisdom to understand that often it is us.

A place where we face our fear of failure. Where we confront that Caledonian cringe which merely reinforces doubt. Where we are not prisoners of our past, but the cause of what happens next.

This is the place where Scotland's horizons should be stretched, not squeezed.

This is the Parliament which we have all helped to shape, and which will now shape us and our children's future.

Our new legislature, as our first First Minister Donald Dewar put it, is not an end in itself. It is simply a means to greater ends.

For it is at Holyrood, in Donald's words, that we Scots of this and future generations, will say 'who we are and how we carry ourselves'.

Rt. Hon. George Reid MSP
Presiding Officer

Devolving Scotland
David McCrone

Prologue

'The Scottish Parliament, which adjourned on 25 March in the year 1707 is hereby reconvened.'

Winnie Ewing MSP, opening the first session of the Parliament, May 1999

Recall

I have recalled the Scottish Parliament
From hatbands and inlaid drawers,
From glazed insides of earthenware teapots,
Corners of greenhouses, tumblers
Where it has lain in session too long,
Not defunct but slurring its speeches
In a bleary, irresolute tirade
Affronting the dignity of the house,
Or else exiled to public transport
For late-night sittings, the trauchled members
Slumped in wee rows either side of the chamber
Girning on home through the rain.
My aunt died, waiting for this recall
In her Balfron cottage. I want her portrait
Hung with those of thousands of others
Who whistled the auld sang toothily under their breath.
Let her be painted full-length, upright

In her anorak, flourishing secateurs.
She knew the MPs in funny wigs
Would return bareheaded after their long recess
To relearn and slowly unlearn themselves,
Walking as if in boyhood and girlhood
They'd just nipped down to the shops for the messages
And taken the winding path back.

Robert Crawford in *Masculinity* (Jonathan Cape, London, 1996.
Reprinted with the kind permission of the publisher and the author.)

Hindsight works wonders. Would Scotland have built its Parliament
if it had known then what it knows now? Probably not. Should it have
done so? Indubitably yes. Many of the key decisions in the life of a nation
depend less on careful and considered judgement, and more – more often
than we like to admit – on happenstance, serendipity, and sheer bloody-
mindedness. 'There shall be a Scottish Parliament. I like that.' said Donald
Dewar, on whom the title father of the nation sat, like his suits, ill at ease.
It was the combined vision of this awkward, accomplished and deeply
cultured man with the quixotic, sometime infuriating, dream of the
Catalan, Enric Miralles, which gave it birth, and which left the rest of
us working it through, defending its costs, filling in the spaces.

In the Beginning

Holyrood was nowhere to be seen: there was a palace, and a brewery.
In the initial months after the referendum of 1997 when three-quarters
of Scots said 'yes' to the principle, and, maybe remarkably, two-thirds
assented to differential tax-varying powers, it seemed to be down to a
competition between Calton Hill, the old Royal High School building,
and a new-build at Victoria Quay in Leith. Somehow a railway yard at

Haymarket came, and just as quickly, went. By early 1998, Holyrood had come from nowhere and got Donald's vote, ostensibly for the bargain basement sum of £40m, a price ticket that would haunt his successors for a long time to come. Calton Hill was too small, and anyway, it was said, a Labour politician had proclaimed it a 'nationalist shibboleth', thus guaranteeing SNP support and Labour hostility from then on: odd, really, for it was Labour who had refurbished it in the 1970s in expectation of the 'assembly' which never came, and defended it with the fervour of the recently converted in the dark days of the 1980s when all seemed lost.

All politics contains mythology, and none more so than the Scottish variety. There is, for example, the view that Holyrood was *got up* on the Edinburgh to Glasgow train in September 1997, when a surveyor fell into the company of travelling civil servants discussing a site for the Parliament building, and casually mentioned to them that a client might just have a site to suit. Then there is the accusation that Holyrood was the result of an aversion to Calton Hill on the grounds of its 'shibboleth' status. This is a curious one, because no one has owned up to it, though the leader of the Scottish National Party, Alex Salmond, has his suspicions, telling the Holyrood Inquiry: 'It is not a word that somebody would just take, as it were, off the shelf. It is the word that would be used by an erudite person, which maybe narrows the field somewhat'. He goes on '. . . Alternatively, Donald is one of the few people who might use a word like 'shibboleth'. I do not know; I have no knowledge, apart from it appeared' (Holyrood Inquiry: para 237, 13 November 2003).[1]

There is also the matter of the figure of £40m which has become a benchmark set in stone, even though evidence laid before the Holyrood Inquiry indicates that in the early months of 1999 it was more than double that once VAT, fees, contingencies, IT and temporary accommodation were taken into account (statement to the Holyrood Inquiry by Donald

Dewar's pps, MS-9-001). Sir David Steel, who was the Parliament's first Presiding Officer, testified to the Inquiry that declared cost at handover (June 1999) was at least £109m (Holyrood Inquiry, MS-12-003). In truth, £40m would have bought very little, perhaps a modest office block for a town council, which many feared, and some hoped for: kill Home Rule by limiting its vision, diminishing its purpose; suitable for a peedie, pretendy parliament, some sneered. Instead, Scotland got its visionary Parliament because its leaders, as well as its people, were thrawn: good money poured after good, because there was, in truth, no alternative, at least once the process had begun. This, after all, is a Parliament: it is not an assembly. It makes laws for the people of Scotland; it rules over matters of key importance to them; it is not their only Parliament, but it is the one that matters most to them.

A City of Parliaments

How, then, are we to read this building? What does it signify? Why is it even here? The short answer is that we have it because it is the express wish of the Scottish people. We asked for it. We did not quite ask for it in the form in which it came, but we asked for it nonetheless. It is ours. It belongs to Scotland. Scot-land. Miralles knew there was something elemental about that land. Elegiacally he observed: 'our proposal is that Scotland is a land, not a series of cities. It demands a construction that is not monumental in the classical sense'. This was not going to be some ersatz baronial confection in the park, a mock gothic edifice which, to some, was how a parliament ought to look. It was to be confected out of upturned boats, out of leaves and twigs, and the sceptics mocked. What nonsense: what does he know of us, they asked? Besides, the land of mountain and the flood would soon wash these elements – those boats, leaves, twigs – away. Let us have, they said, something with pillars and pilasters, if not a Pugin-esque little brother, at least something Grand and Scottish. 'Something more traditional would be better', said Nigel Tranter, who wrote popular history books. The successor to the throne, the Duke of Rothesay, let his views be known that the palace next door was wanting a suitable foil of similar marque. They did not get it, and Scotland, one might add, is the better for it.

The puzzle, though, is this: how do you build a parliament for the twenty-first century, not the nineteenth, and, to boot, a parliament for an understated nation? How do you create an institution with so many conflicting demands in a country – a capital city, indeed, with three other parliament buildings already? The short answer is that all three belong to other worlds, other times. Edinburgh has the grandeur of Parliament Hall, now patrolled by peripatetic advocates and their clients, but in essence a creation of a pre-democratic patrician age: a parliament for the landed elite ruling Scotland into the 1707 Union, an erstwhile parcel of rogues in that nation. Then there is the ill-fated 'shibboleth' on Calton Hill, the old Royal High School, the Parthenon model designed by Thomas Hamilton in the late 1820s, described as 'one of the setpieces of archaeological Hellenism in Europe'.[2] To some, it looks like a parliament; it feels like one, if the model is that of nineteenth-century bourgeois nationalism, an edifice for an emerging class wresting power from a landed aristocracy, but hardly one for the complex twenty-first century world. In Jonathan Hearn's words: 'It was a style that expressed the rationalism and austere liberalism of the governing classes of eighteenth and nineteenth-century Scotland, especially in Edinburgh'.[3]

Why, then, some asked, not make do with the Assembly Hall on the Mound, already acting as temporary home until the new one is ready? Why did we need another one? In short, because it belongs to someone else: a national church, which, in the long years without a parliament, took on the mantle and responsibility to speak for Scotland. This too is history. Further, austere and draughty churches are poor models for the politics of the twenty-first century with their argument and their flyting. Scotland is, for good or ill, no longer a godly realm. In short, the models we have to hand do not fit our needs: Scotland is not ruled by a patrician class, nor by a burgher class, nor by a godly class. Maybe we need a parliament *sans* class; classy, to be sure, but the property of the people, the common weal: a parliament for a new century.

Deciphering Scotland

To answer the question who and what is a parliament for, we need to first ask what Scotland is for. What is this country about? It is a seeming bundle of contradictions. It is one of the oldest nations in Europe, established more or less in its present frontiers a millennium ago, and yet there is an important sense in which it can be said not to exist. Evidently, it is not a state in the fully formal sense of that term. Here we enter a somewhat confusing array of terms. Despite the tendency to use 'state' and 'nation' as synonyms, they actually belong to different conceptual realms. 'State' is, in essence, a political-constitutional term for a self-governing territory. 'Nation', on the other hand, is a cultural concept which is not predicated on political self-governance, but upon the sense of felt distinctiveness; the right, if not the practice, of self-determination. In short, the nation is an 'imagined community', bounded by place, territory, as well as by time, by history.[4] Scotland's people certainly had a sense of themselves as a distinct nation as early as the middle of the fourteenth century, forged in the wars with its larger and more powerful neighbour to the south. Yet it more or less willingly gave up its constitutional independence less than four hundred years later, and embraced union with its auld enemy. In so doing, it transformed itself economically to become the second country in the world to industrialise, and to punch well above its political weight in the context of the greatest empire the world has yet seen.

Why, then, re-invent a parliament given up nigh on three hundred years ago in 1707? A nation once again? Well, no – Scotland has never ceased to be a nation. Scotland is a land, occupied by diverse peoples down through the ages who forged themselves into a community by having sufficient interests in common, and creating social institutions to match, the 'holy trinity' of law, education and religion. But wait, said some: Scots are too like their soudrons, the English, to make that much difference. After all, they speak (a version of) the same language – English; they have been formally Protestant since the middle of the sixteenth-century until it ceased to matter much in the twentieth-century; and above all, they have shared the same state, the United Kingdom, for almost three hundred years. All that is true, but barely touches the issue. Differences like language may, at times, be necessary, but insufficient to explain alternative imagined communities. After all, Americans speak English, and they are not 'English', so why should the Scots be? The point is that Scotland is not England because the imagining process is different, and it is sustained by a different history, culture and set of institutions. True, not being English matters, but only contra – vis-à-vis – not against, at least not since 1707.

A deeper puzzle remains. Why now? Why the recovery of a parliament almost three hundred years after giving it up? The veteran Nationalist, Winnie Ewing, opened the first session of the 1999 Parliament as the 'mother' of the nation, its oldest elected member, by implying that there had simply been a hiatus between 1707 and 1999. The link between the old and the new, the pre-modern and the democratic, the independent and devolved, was made with some elegance, if some historical inexactitude. Following the Union of 1707, Scotland was always something of an anomaly. It had successfully defended itself against England in the wars of independence at the turn of the fourteenth century, before helping to create 'Great Britain' under the Union of Crowns when its king, James VI, succeeded to the English throne in 1603. Just over a century later, Scotland and England combined their legislatures in the Union of Parliaments under a single parliament – in London – to form the basis of the United Kingdom. In this venture, Scotland was certainly not a colony; it had not been conquered by England, unlike its Celtic neighbours, Ireland and Wales. Rather, it successfully sustained its independence before entering as a (junior) partner into a British state on the verge of developing into the most successful empire the world has hitherto seen. The 'auld enemy' – England – became its newest and closest ally, usurping the aulder alliance with France dating back to the thirteenth century.

In truth, the Union was, and remains, a marriage of convenience – *a mariage de raison* – for Scotland. It gave up its parliament at a time when democracy, as we know it, did not exist in exchange for a share in the economic and political spoils of empire, and opportunities for Scots on the make. Our autonomy was underpinned by institutional arrangements which, at the time, mattered more than formal parliamentary democracy. Scotland had its legal, educational and ecclesiastical systems to run its internal, domestic affairs, and as long as these did not interfere with grand affairs of state and empire, then it was left to its own devices. There were occasions such as the Jacobite risings in the eighteenth century which threatened the authority of the British state, and its system of crown succession, but that state had sufficient power to crush the dissidents and ensure that Scotland was safe for the Union.

The anomaly, meanwhile, was quietly embedded into the British state. Simply put, Scotland was autonomous, with control over its domestic affairs, while governed by a single pan-British legislature in London. For most of the history of the two hundred and fifty years after the Union it did not matter much. Even after the advent of universal suffrage which, to all intents and purposes, arrived only in the second decade of the twentieth century, Scotland, unlike Ireland, was a full and peaceful partner in the Union. Not for it a war of liberation, throwing off the yoke of a 'foreign' power, as Ireland had done at the start of the twentieth century. Scotland was different, ironically, because it had fought for and maintained its independence some centuries earlier, had evolved distinctive institutional and cultural ways of doing things, and took advantage of imperial opportunities out of proportion to its size and status as a power. What would have been the point of throwing off the 'English yoke' if Scots were already self-governing, and helping to run the empire? In truth, there was none, at least until the second half of the twentieth century. It was largely the fault of democracy, or to be more precise, majoritarian democracy, the political will of the largest number. Universal suffrage in a state with a single legislature always had the potential for England to assert its numerical superiority over its smaller partners.

In short, the political crisis of the late-twentieth century arose because of the will of the (British) majority. In the single legislature at Westminster, Scots were never going to outnumber English voters, but for much of the twentieth century, it mattered little, for people on both sides of the Tweed voted in similar ways. Only from the 1950s did Scotland and England diverge in their political preferences, a divergence magnified by the vagaries of the electoral system of first-past-the-post. Ultimately, by the late 1970s and 1980s, Scotland got a government England voted for, as it long had done, but by then, it mattered considerably that the ruling party did not have a political mandate in Scotland. So there entered the political lexicon the 'democratic deficit' whereby the political complexion of the British House of Commons was coloured by an English hue regardless of how Scots voted. This translated into a Conservative majority built upon English votes. The final quarter of the twentieth century saw the emergence of a Nationalist party committed to ending the Union and taking Scotland back into formal independence. Faced with Unionism and Nationalism, the dying Labour government of 1979 sought, in some panic, to introduce an 'assembly' for Scotland (and one for Wales), and while a majority of Scots who voted in a referendum in that year voted yes (52%, to 48% against), it was insufficient to overcome rules rigged by opponents of constitutional change who forced the minority government to set a 40% hurdle such that this percentage of the electorate (not those actually voting) had to approve before the bill was passed. That Labour government was swept from power later that year, and a unionist Conservative party held sway for the next 18 years.

There followed long years of agitation across a wide spectrum of political and social opinion for constitutional change to come about. Labour, initially suspicious of devolution as the thin edge of a constitutional wedge, became a cautious convert to the cause of Home Rule, of a quasi-federal United Kingdom, recognising the distinctive national polities of the non-English territories. The 1979 debacle had persuaded the constitutional middle ground of Scottish politics that neither the status quo of the Union, nor formal independence was the answer. Instead, there was a revival of the concept of 'Home Rule' invented at the end of the nineteenth century, ironically for Ireland, which left the Union when this modest reform was not delivered.

The language of the late-twentieth century spoke not of Home Rule but of 'devolution', of power delegated by Westminster to the lower tiers of government: power perhaps devolved, but power theoretically retained at the centre. This, though, was not quite how people in Scotland saw it. The recovery of a parliament in Edinburgh did not imply that the building on the banks of the Thames was paramount, even though it had the power to prorogue the powers of the devolved parliament if it saw fit. It was theoretically possible, but in practice impossible to do, for what was won in the referendum of 1997 was a stepwise shift in self-government, a move further along the spectrum of political autonomy. Scotland's parliament was seen to be a recovery of the old one, not the acceptance of agency status to carry out the wishes of Westminster.

Above all, unlike 1979, it was a *parliament*, not an *assembly*, with those powers not explicitly reserved to Westminster being implicitly devolved to Holyrood. Unlike Wales, the Scottish parliament had the power to make primary law. Indeed, what had persuaded some erstwhile opponents of Home Rule to convert to the cause had been the fact that Westminster could not adequately handle Scottish legislation, passing only a couple of bills a year at the tail-end of parliamentary business. In contrast, the Scottish parliament passed over sixty bills in its first full four-year session.

Has the Scottish anomaly been solved? Yes and no; yes, insofar as a directly elected Scottish Parliament is at liberty, within the remit of the Scotland Act, to elect the government it wants and to pass the legislation it thinks fit: no, insofar as new anomalies are built into the constitutional system, notably that the Westminster Parliament has to double up both as a UK and an English legislature, with Scottish (and Welsh) members being able to vote on purely English matters, and, of course, having no direct say in domestic affairs governing their own constituents (what became known as the West Lothian question after MP Tam Dalyell whose seat that once was). There is also the fact that most Scots, while recognising the primacy of Westminster as the more influential institution as far as Scotland is concerned, also think that Holyrood *should* be the more important of the two. In other words, there may be constitutional clarification, but in terms of sociological understanding, the relationship between the two parliaments is not clear in the mind of Scots. If what matters most to them are 'home' affairs – schools, housing, jobs – then the focus falls naturally on Holyrood rather than Westminster.

Politics in the 21st Century

There, however, is a bigger picture to consider. We are not dealing in zero-sum games here; winners do not take all any more. Even to suggest that one has to choose which level is paramount seems to fly in the face of what life is like in the twenty-first century, for power does not reside in one place. In short, it is both layered and shared. Europe, Britain, Scotland – we live in a multi-level world of inter-connecting spheres of influence. The language of 'sovereignty', the primacy of one level over the others, does not ring true. Instead, we have much more subtle and nuanced power relations; of open, not closed government. To be sure, the language of constitutional politics is still largely that of absolutes: if *they* have power, *we* won't have any, but that is largely a matter of an inherited political vocabulary derived from the nineteenth century. This old language spoke in capital letters and loud voices; We, The People; the Democratic Will. The trouble is that people do not listen very carefully any more. Our age is one of lower-case, softly spoken, mixed messages. Politics as a trade is held in low esteem, for there are limits to political achievement these days. The irony is that the Scottish Parliament has come along precisely at a time of maximum difficulty for democratic institutions. Our representatives are told: do something, and as quickly as possible, and they more or less accede, for it is a brave politician who replies, in the face of demands, that life is much more complicated than the questioner implies.

We also live in an age in which the vocabulary of democracy is used more and more, but opportunities to implement it are ever more constrained. Above all, the global culture of the marketplace implies that everyone has equal right of access to what they want, but actually conspires to limit choices, judging them appropriate only in the context of the ability to pay the price. Hence, the democracy of the marketplace is a contradiction in terms, for the market delivers, and depends on, inequalities of people's life chances, not their constitutional right to be treated equally. The dilemma for politics in the twenty-first century is that the extension of the market has reduced its power for manoeuvre and, to deliver services on the basis of need rather than the ability to pay, while at the same time the 'consumer' demands more from their political leaders who find it, in turn, difficult to deliver. In short, the language of the 'customer' has superseded, or at best constrained, that of 'citizen'.

The Scottish Parliament has been born into this culture of contradictory expectations. In the first place, it is a devolved institution with control over 'domestic' matters, and without the even limited panoply of powers over macro-economic and constitutional matters, such as they are. Secondly, it comes in to a world deeply sceptical of the political craft, and yet one overly demanding on its elected representatives to 'do something'. We can see in the short life of our Parliament something of how these contradictions play out. The Parliament was born in a wave of high expectations. Much has been made of the alleged fact that these expectations of the Parliament in 1997 have been dashed, that the brave new Scotland has failed to materialise in the first four years of its life. In truth, the picture is much more complex. First of all, devolution is the only game in town. Only 1 in 10 want a return to the status quo ante where Scotland was governed directly from London. Around 1 in 4 want some form of independence, most in the context of a Scotland as a full member of the European Union. The majority of Scots, around 6 in 10, prefer a devolved Scottish parliament to either of these options, and this indubitably has become the new status quo.

We know from our studies of public opinion since 1997 that people in Scotland want a parliament, not so much as an end in itself, an expression of their national identity, but as a means of making a better Scotland in which to live and work.[5] In other words, the vehicle for policy changes was to be the Parliament and a devolved government, and in broad terms there has been a decline in people's expectations during the first four years of the Parliament's existence. Much, for example, has been made of surveys showing that there has been a fall in the number of people over this period expecting improvements in Scotland's economy, and standards in the health service (roughly, from two-thirds to less than a half), and an even greater one as regards the quality of education. These headline changes, however, conceal more subtle ones, namely, that people have levelled down expectations rather than moved to outright hostility. Further, rightly or wrongly, they blame this downturn on Westminster rather than on Holyrood, which receives the plaudits among those judging that things have got better. In short, the electorate does not believe that actually having a parliament has made things worse, merely that devolution has not had the immediate pay-off they had initially hoped for in those first few euphoric months. While devolution has not had quite the immediate impact on policy outcomes, there is little evidence that the whole political project of Home Rule has been undermined. Indeed, the most common response to disappointment with the Scottish Parliament is to demand that it is given *more* political powers, not fewer.[6]

The downsizing of expectations appears to be happening across most of the western world, and not simply in Scotland, or the United Kingdom. There is fairly widespread disenchantment with the political elites in most countries, as well as with the capacity of political parties to deliver. In other words, the decline in political trust and the efficacy of the system is fairly endemic and it is Scotland's (mis)fortune to find itself caught up in this tide. While most Scots recognise that Westminster is in practice a more powerful parliament than Holyrood, they consistently prefer (by a majority of 4 to 1) that Holyrood was the more powerful; hardly evidence that the whole devolution project has run into the sand. Indeed, the differential between trusting Edinburgh over London remains at a broadly similar ratio of 3 to 1 even though the absolute numbers trusting either tier of government has diminished. With hindsight, the late 1990s was a period of unusually high expectations among the UK electorate as a whole, as a discredited Conservative government was swept from office, with the ruling party managing to return no MPs whatsoever in both Scotland and Wales, thus paving the way for constitutional change on a hitherto unforeseen scale in British politics.

Holyrood Stanes

In Walter Scott's novel, *Heart of Midlothian*, Mrs Howden complains: 'I ken, when we had a King, and a chancellor and Parliament – men o' our ain, we could aye peeble them wi' stanes when they werena gude bairns – But naebody's nails can reach the length o' Lunnon.' Scott's character, Mrs Howden, was complaining that she and her neighbours did not have the satisfaction of witnessing the hanging of Captain Porteous, whose soldiers had fired on the Edinburgh mob. Thankfully, the death penalty has been abolished, but the appeal of the quotation to many contemporary commentators, frequently out of context, is that Scots are deemed to be intimate with their politicians, and, at least metaphorically, to be able to peeble them with stanes. While Scottish parliamentarians since 2003 have not exactly been pelted with stones in the Lawnmarket, they have not been showered in bouquets either. Much of this is, in truth, unfair. There has never been a political institution which, in the full glare of publicity, has had to grow up so quickly. Its founding principles – sharing power,

accountability, access and participation, and equality of opportunity –
ensured that it set for itself the stiffest of examinations. There must have
been politicians who regretted making the Parliament such an open and
accessible place, especially in the face of a critical and competitive press.
Those who came from Westminster with its douce and arcane rules and
procedures, rarely open to public gaze, probably never recovered from
the shock of adapting to the twenty-first century,

The building of the new Scottish Parliament at Holyrood became,
it seems, something of a lightning conductor for general political
disenchantment. Nailing an ill-thought out £40m price-tag to the mast
was always going to make life more difficult than it already was, and
appreciating building costs have been, in truth, too good a political story
for the media not to run with. Nevertheless, who carries that particular
can is not at all clear. Thus, a survey in July 2003 suggested that the
electorate were not prepared to blame any single individual or group.[7]
The political class of MSPs were deemed most at blame, followed by the
contractors, then Westminster/The Treasury, architects and civil servants,
with Donald Dewar and the present First Minister, Jack McConnell, taking
up the rear. On the other hand, a clear majority of people were prepared
to agree with the view that 'when the project is completed, Scotland will
have a parliament building of which it can be proud', and only about one-
third dissenting. The Scottish Social Attitudes survey of 2003 confirmed
this ambivalence. Opinion was fairly evenly spread between those who
thought it should never have been built (46%), and those who thought it
was needed but that it was too costly (45%), with 7% supporting the view
that it would all be worth it in the end. To complicate matters, fully half
of those who said that it should never have been built also wanted the
Parliament to have more powers. One is reminded of Walt Whitman's
comment: 'Do I contradict myself? Very well then I contradict myself,

(I am large, I contain multitudes.)' ('Song of Myself' 1855). What these data suggest is that Scots are at worst ambivalent, and at best, sophisticated, about the political project of Home Rule and its embodiment in the Holyrood building.

The focus on a 'value for money' debate is an interesting one, because behind it lies important issues of social as well as economic worth. It is in fact a debate confusing value with cost, and it is interesting that political opponents of the whole devolution project, once the battle to prevent it happening had been lost, have sought to reduce its power and symbolism. The initial guesstimate of £40m appears to have been little more than a rough stab at what it would cost to build an extension to the Scottish Office at Victoria Quay, Leith. The leader of the Conservative Party in the Scottish Parliament cited a letter from the then Permanent Secretary in the Scottish Office to the effect that 'The £40m figure related to a new build (at Leith) on a brownfield site to a reasonable modern standard' (*The Scotsman*, 20 August 2003). His reaction is interesting: 'That proposal sounded reasonable to me at the time, and it sounds even better now. We could have had an Asda-price Parliament – the politicians responsible for making the key decisions chose not to.' The gulf between a shopping centre model and a custom-built parliament could not be better expressed. Tagging an office-block alongside the headquarters of the Scottish civil service is perhaps indicative of the value placed upon devolution, subsumed under the issue of cost. 'Value for money' has become a code-phrase in the neo-liberal lexicon for low-cost, as well as the use of private financing on a low budget. Building a parliament complex with a minimum life of one hundred years is quite a different matter altogether.

The rise in costs derives from a number of factors: primarily an inconsistency between the original guesstimates of cost (£10–40m in the White Paper), and their alignment with a brief which resonated with the requirement to create a landmark; the transfer of patronage from the Executive to the Parliament; the subsequent re-appraisal of the brief resulting in a doubling of the required floor spaces to some 33,000sqm; the prolongation of the design and construction phases caused by this; and the development and resolution of blast protection. All this has given critics something of a field day, notably those sections of the media who were hostile to the whole Home Rule project from the outset, and who found it less easy to attack the project after the 1997 referendum gave it overwhelming backing. There are those keen to point out that one could get so many hospitals/schools for the money, but these tend to be political critics who were never very keen on public investment at all.

Those supportive of the project pointed out the long history of overspend of such projects: in recent years, the Greenwich Dome, Portcullis House, an office block adjacent to the palace of Westminster which came in at £250m, and the British Library which ran out at £400m, three times the original cost. Those with longer historical memories recalled the overspends on Wren's St Paul's Cathedral and Pugin's Houses of Parliament. The journalist George Rosie commented wryly:

> *Holyrood's delays are as nothing to those that bedevilled Westminster. There were 33 years between the start of the work on the coffer dam in 1837 to the finishing touches in 1870. That's three decades of rows, public sackings, government inquiries, strikes, political interference and cost overruns. All of them set against a background of attacks from publicity-seeking MPs, discontented architects, outraged aesthetes and a press which then, as now, likes nothing more than a rammy in high places.*
> *The Sunday Herald*, 1 February 2004

The taxpayer ended up paying £3m (£150m at today's prices), five times the original estimate. Neither did it escape the notice of some that many of the most spectacular overspends were on London projects. Nationalists in particular found it difficult to be too critical of the project in the light of these spends. If such costly projects were good enough for London then they felt honour-bound to support a suitably expensive Scottish Parliament, while carping at the manner in which spending had risen. Sydney Opera House provides an example that such projects are not all British and that ultimately cost considerations can be overtaken by the cultural and architectural symbolism of the building.

There is, however, a more fundamental and interesting issue behind the apparent receding popularity of the Parliament, and that relates to the 'ownership' of the institution. Put simply, whose Parliament is it anyway? This is a serious question which grows out of the long process of Home Rule. The failure of Westminster parties to deliver devolution – and let us remember that a majority voted yes in the 1979 referendum – meant that it was left to civil society to agitate for the Parliament. The twenty-year campaign since 1979 was waged by a motley crew of campaigners and civil associations from trade unions to churches to women's groups, all unelected, but all donning the mantle of speaking for Scotland. Some parliamentarians like to think that as elected representatives, they alone represent the nation, but that is not how the nation sees it. Parliament became the people's forum, on loan to the political class, as long as they treated it, and them, with some respect, given the partiality of politics in the twenty-first century. Power sharing – between government, parliament and people – is a three-way system, and not the preserve of any single agent. The Scottish doctrine of 'popular sovereignty' juxtaposed against 'crown sovereignty' as practised at Westminster may be more of an aspiration than a legal principle, but nonetheless, it gels with the view that politics, and the Parliament, isn't everything. The people are paramount.

Parliament as brickbat reflects how quickly and deeply it has embedded itself in Scottish life. In its short but eventful existence, it has become the institution to be talked about, though not always in a complimentary way. In truth, it is a remarkable institution. It is much more representative of Scottish society than one could have imagined; it has one of the highest proportions of women members (37%) in the western world; it has a multi-party system which places it in the mainstream of European politics: a social democratic party, a regionalist/nationalist one, a centre Liberal Party, a right of centre Conservative Party, a socialist one, and a Green. In short, it is a rainbow parliament, from red to blue, with all shades in between, including tartan. It has a coalition government which circumvents the notorious elective dictatorships which Westminster usually produces. Despite having limited powers, the Parliament has carved out distinctive policies: abolishing upfront tuition fees for students, repealing homophobic legislation, introducing free personal care for the elderly, passing land reform legislation, along with over sixty bills in the first session of Parliament.

A Parliament for a Future

So what sort of parliament has been built at the start of the new millennium? What is the grammar, syntax and vocabulary of Holyrood? Andy MacMillan, friend and professional colleague of Enric Miralles, and one of the judges for the competition, observed that the new parliament had to be 'dynamic, interactive, transparent, in the spirit of open government; a public building of international significance owned by the nation in an appropriate public setting. Not a rented-back commercial investment in some developer's urban package'. Miralles himself observed that the purpose of the building was to mediate between town and land.

The classical project of the nineteenth century saw parliaments as tabernacles, sacred groves tended by a professional priesthood equipped with esoteric rituals. The people could look, but they could not touch, and rarely did they understand what was going on, nor were they encouraged to. They could worship from the back, but were forbidden to approach the inner tabernacle. This is the image of Corinthian columns, gothic cathedrals, please-keep-off-the-grass, not for the likes of you. This is the expression of the grand narrative of modernity, rather than the *bricolage* of the twenty-first century.

To caricature, modern vocabularies are quite different:

old	new
imperial	domestic
closed	open
top-down	bottom-up
transmitting	receiving
command	reflect
power	legitimacy
town	land
monument	anent humanity

Miralles tried to express this in his architecture. He described his work as 'very removed from the task of representing ideal situations', characterised by 'strange shapes . . . dimensions so far from any ideal . . . different topographies'. Miralles likened his projects to 'designs in the weave of a carpet', calling for 'repeated actions: a series of movement flows which unite these works, creating common themes, reconciling individual situations, mixing different programs, and extending every construction to form a series of relationships with its surroundings'.[8] Many have observed Miralles' liking for the work of Charles Rennie Mackintosh who, in the words of one commentator, 'did not just absorb the potential of plant forms as a source of applied ornament; the principles of their formal evolution informed his designs'.[9]

The site itself is crucial to Miralles' design. He commented: 'we don't want to forget that the Scottish Parliament will be in Edinburgh, but it will belong to Scotland, to the Scottish Land'. His key idea was that the Scottish Parliament mediated between town and land, and he sought to avoid it translating into a fortress of power. This openness derived not simply from the lines of the site itself, but from the ambivalence with which Scotland as a whole viewed the Edinburgh Parliament. It happens to be in Edinburgh, but it belongs to Scotland. Capture must be avoided; its symbolism opens up to the iconography of the land. And not only the land: the sea. In the words of the poet Kathleen Jamie, 'an upturned boat – a watershed'.[10]

Decoding Holyrood

The site itself is a central part of this message. It is not simply the complex of buildings which gives the Parliament its power, but the resonances of the landscape. In truth, this is a powerful place with multiple and evocative layerings of meaning. Put simply, this cruciform (holy-rood, after all is the holy cross) is a diagrammatic representation of four of the key bases of power in any society: military, political, cultural, commercial.

The historic source of power is best represented by force or military might, in this instance, by the castle. Here is top-down – 'high' – power architecturally expressed by the symbol of the fortress, dominating the cityscape: high state power, reinforced by distance on the hill. The limitations of 'force', better perhaps captured by 'might', in German *macht*, derive from its naked and overbearing qualities.[11] To work, might has frequently to be present, to impinge directly on the powerless. When coercion is absent, it is difficult to enforce obedience.

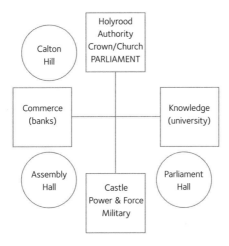

The coercive capacity of military might is terrifying as long as its agents are able to lay hands on the subjects. Alice's Red Queen, after all, was only powerful if her soldiers had heads to chop off. Power, in other words and in this context, is despotic rather than diffused.

At the other end, the bottom end of the High Street, lie much more subtle, diffused and longer-lasting forms of power, what we might call 'authority', or 'low' power, in German, *herrschaft*. This is power cloaked or disguised by legitimacy such that people obey its strictures when it is neither obvious nor present. It represents a much more nuanced and intimate form of power – domestic and domesticated. 'Authority' inculcates obedience by becoming routinised through social institutions. In medieval times, this was symbolised through the power of the church, or by obedience to the royal personage of the monarchy, the traditional source of charismatic authority. People obey, in other words, because in some real sense they want to, because it matters to them, rather than because they are coerced. What we find at the foot of the High Street are historic layers of such power: church, king, and now parliament.

The metaphor which comes readily to mind is palimpsest, originally referring to writing parchment used and re-used, whereby the imprints of one age are overlain on an other, thereby producing a layering of cultures and meanings. The surface is used and re-used to suit the needs and aspirations of the present without eradicating entirely what was there before, which seeps through, as it were, leaving its footprint for others to follow. There is nothing inevitable about this process, however. We gang our ain gyte in the landscape, but we frequently fall in with the steps of those who have gone before us. That is nicely captured in physical space at 'Holyrood', first an abbey, and then a palace, and now in the twenty-first century, a parliament: church, king, polity – layer upon layer, drawing up from below the meanings of previous ages and refashioning them for the new. In the middle ages, Holyrood was also a place of sanctuary, religious, criminal and latterly for debtors, whereby those within its boundaries were protected from the authorities.[12] Holyrood was one of the largest sanctuaries in Scotland, its girth running round all of Arthur's Seat to the edge of Duddingston Loch. Within its confines people could take refuge, and even set up residence on payment of a fee to the Baillie who controlled life therein. This was no lawless place, but strictly controlled and managed. The system of protection was not abolished until the end of the nineteenth century, though it is claimed that sanctuary rights in Holyrood Park have never been formally repealed. 'It is said that the Park is still a place of sanctuary for debtors and the office of Baillie still exists, though whether the modern system and organisations such as the Inland Revenue would take a benign eye of our old rights and traditions seems doubtful'.[13]

All this helps to impart a sense of mystique to the site of Holyrood, a sacral space in anthropological terms within which the normal rules of social conduct do not seem to apply in quite the way they do elsewhere. It is symbolic territory, sacred space, in which certain key rituals and activities are carried out. The symbolism of Holyrood, the layering of its sources of power through the ages, means that it is a much more potent site than, say, an extension to an office block on a brownfield dockland site at Leith. Holyrood has the power to conjure up magic, is able to draw-up to itself the symbols and associations surrounding it. In short, the charisma lies partly in the site itself, in its historical and geographic associations. It is coupled with new-build which might harness the old, but is not dependent upon it. In a lecture at the Edinburgh Festival in August 2003, the recently -retired Presiding Officer of the Scottish Parliament, Sir David Steel, remarked that the late First Minister, Donald Dewar, had commented to him: 'Don't you think, David, that a new Scottish Parliament after an absence of 300 hundred years merits a new building and not just a jumble of old ones?' (*The Herald*, 19 August 2003). An unusually literate and well-read politician like Dewar was not proposing a modern office block because it was functional and cheap; he was recognising the powerful symbolism of synthesising the power of the new and the patina of the old. In her testimony to the Holyrood Inquiry, the broadcaster Kirsty Wark, who was one of the competition judges, observed: '. . . I think his [Donald Dewar's] overriding concern was to get a landmark, a great building for Scotland, for the people of Scotland. I do not think he had any arrogance about what his contribution was going to be. And I certainly do not think he wanted a grand building; grand was never in it. He wanted a landmark building; he wanted something that suggested a new modern Scotland'.[14] In the case of the parliamentary complex, of course, the old – in the form of Queensberry House – was incorporated into the fabric.[15]

The Parliament should not simply be seen on a vertical axis on the High Street, but also on the horizontal. Here, it draws upon the two other sources of power and legitimacy, commerce and education: money and knowledge, symbolised by the proximity of the headquarters of Scotland's (and Europe's) two major banks, Royal Bank of Scotland and HBOS (Bank of Scotland/Halifax), and of the University of Edinburgh. Indeed, Miralles liked to refer to his parliament complex as a 'campus', a cloister for reasoned debate and argument, a debating chamber for measured deliberation and decision. In his sketchbook, Miralles wrote:

> *I imagine that a Parliament should be organised like a university campus. A special kind of knowledge is produced . . . Parliaments need to be different places where to think, to walk . . . The Palace should not be the model. The Dome should not be the model.*

He was also influenced by Le Corbusier, and in particular his chapel at Ronchamp. This can be most easily seen in the public space entrance hall, evocative of cathedral (crosses on the ceiling) and railway station/meeting space.

The Parliament is open to the elements, looking up to Salisbury Crags, and the Radical Road in particular: in that respect, more political symbolism. The road was conceived by Walter Scott and his friends in the 1820s as a project to employ (radical) weavers who had been dispossessed by economic and technological change, and who became a political symbol for radicals down through the ages. Exiting the Parliament, one's eyes are drawn up to the Crags and the Radical Road, a reminder of the continuities between past and present. Parliament is not simply built on the outcrop, but symbolises the outcrop, the locale for jostling, arguing, flyting, contradicting.[16] The building complex is also designed to be seen from above, for the roofscapes with their distinctive boats motif are a vital part of the design. In other words, this is a building designed to be seen, not simply used. In Scotland we are never far away from elemental landscape, and it plays a central part in our imaginings about identity. In the Highlands, for example, the Gaelic concept of *duthchas* implies the notion of collective heritage, of a hereditary, elemental, connection to the land. Much of the controversy about land has derived from a sense of the indissoluble and inalienable right of people to the land on which they have lived and worked.[17]

'Country', too, carries its own set of meanings. The cultural sociologist Raymond Williams pointed out that: '"country" can mean both a nation and part of a land; the "country" can be the whole society as well as its rural area. In the long history of human settlements, this connection between the land from which directly or indirectly we all get our living and the achievements of human society has been deeply known'. 'Country' in other words, has come to stand for the essential values and images of place, hence the fusion of land and nation. Further, national identity frequently depends on an association with landscape, topography mapped, elaborated and enriched as homeland. More specifically, we think of Scotland as a landscape of the mind, a place of the imagination (though certainly not imaginary). Nations have imagined geographies acting as representations of the country. In other words, 'nature' and 'nation' are intimately linked.

It is no accident, then, that Enric Miralles caught this sense of attachment to land in the building, not only in mediating between town and land, but in Land, in the sense that this was to be a parliament for all Scots who inhabited the space of Scot-land. This has older cultural and political resonances, for embedded in Scottish identity is the sense of belonging not to a tribe and ethnic group, but a place, a territory. There is useful irony here too in the fact that eligibility to vote in Scottish parliamentary elections is more open than for Westminster, defined as it is as a 'local' election, and hence open to those who are residents rather than citizens. If you live here, you belong here.

Defining 'Scots' in territorial rather than ethnic terms is the reflection of a long history of a country regionally, culturally, and ethnically diverse. There were many different ways of being a Scot, and only the crown, the monarch, had that capacity to impose a shared identity. That is why there is the tradition of referring to the monarch as king/queen of Scots, rather than 'of Scotland'.[18] It was the early monarchy, most obviously at the time of the Wars of Independence, which became the rallying institution, the symbol of popular sovereignty, but always on a contingent basis. After all, the famous declaration of Arbroath of 1320 was careful to tell the monarch that if he/she did not do the will of the people, they would seek out another who would. The declaration is best remembered for its declamatory words: 'For as long as but a hundred of us remain alive we will never submit to English rule. For it is not for honour and glory for which we fight but freedom, for which no man loses except with his life.' What is revealing is the statement immediately preceding: 'Yet if he [the King] give up what he has begun, seeking to make us or our kingdom subject to the king of England or to the English, we would strive at once to drive him out as an enemy and a subverter of his own right and ours, and we would make some other man who is able to defend us our king.' In short, we will accept you if you do our will. If not, not. Thus, there is a body of history and constitutional theory, which derives authority less from the crown and more from the people. The monarch has legitimacy insofar as he/she conforms to, and expresses, the will of the people. Why should this delving into constitutional history matter? It does so because this is a parliament for a particular kind of people. At the opening of the Parliament in July 1999, Donald Dewar said: 'This is about more than our politics and our laws. This is about who we are, how we carry ourselves.' We draw-up our own history and traditions, our sense of self, and embed them in the fabric of our new Parliament.

Epilogue: Roots and Routes

Buildings are not simply bricks and mortar. Behind the controversy over cost, size, completion dates, is a much more significant symbolic battle over what Scotland is and where it is going. Those who fear the break-up of Britain recognise in their own way this symbolism. If the Parliament has limited powers, is housed in a modern office-block cum shopping centre, then its power to represent as well as to re-present is significantly curtailed. It is very unlikely to carry the force, the power, to act as a focus for change. In this sense, buildings are not inert, not simply the outcomes of decisions; they have the power to signify and move to political action. They energise by remaking our sense of being a people. Throughout history, political change has frequently involved the capture and occupation, sometimes symbolic, often actual, of key sites: castles, parliaments, palaces and squares. Enric Miralles and Donald Dewar knew in their bones the power of place, both as an expression of what had been, but above all the power to move, to change, to transform. Miralles used his leaves and twigs motif in a highly symbolic way, to evoke fluidity and movement, of parliament running into the land, into Scot-land. We are dealing here with a terrain of power, the power to charge, to move to action. This Parliament is a hinge between our past, present and future. Crucially, it connects roots and routes: reaching deep into the past, reading the signs and symbols, but projecting forward into the future, offering signposts on a journey to an undetermined future. It is this power to move, to transform, to stand for what we wish it to signify. This is not an administrative office block, but the democratic crucible in which Scotland's future will ultimately be decided, and on a map as yet unwritten.

Deliverance Comes
Alan Balfour

'There is a great storm coming, which shall try your foundations, Scotland must be rid of Scotland before the deliverance comes.'
James Renwick

> *At the end of most streets of Edinburgh's Old Town rises the crimson wall of Salisbury Craigs a lesson in the unimaginable forces and lapses of time which have gone to shape the world. The Craigs are a basalt intrusion, a fossil tide of volcanic rock which surged through the foundations of a dead volcano some 200 million years ago. Geology and palaeontology, with their revelations of deep time and alien life-forms, towered up wherever 19th century Scots turned their eyes. The 'testimony of the rocks' threatened their moral universe, its narrative incompatible with a creation myth or even with a creator . . . Old Edinburgh is shaped like a gigantic lecture theatre with the end wall covered by a chart of the earth's origins.'* [19]
> *Stone Voices*, Neal Ascherson

The new Parliament of Scotland is the most recent stratum in the wake of this fossil tide, and the most human. It is an original and significant work of public architecture – a work of world distinction. In conceptual ambition and visceral presence it has no equal in Scottish history.

At the presentation that awarded the commission the architect Enric Miralles stated his fundamental concept: 'the building should originate from the sloping base of Arthur's Seat and arrive into the city almost out of the rock'.[20] In an interview given when the Scottish Parliament was much in his mind, Miralles described the way he thought about building, 'you're not just working with the physical reality of the moment, but with the physical reality of everything that has been there as well, or that has built up the place'.[21]

Architecture has a wider and longer lasting influence than any other art form. Works of national architecture are explicitly constructed to last centuries and are always in performance. Fashion, fate and the market determine the life of a work of music, of a painting or sculpture or writing for the theatre.[22] Rarely in the commissioning of a work of art is there an explicit demand for permanence and even more rarely is it asked to embody lasting values that will affect and shape national identity.[23] In its highest form this is the task for architecture.[24]

This new Parliament is shaped to be inspiration and instrument, stage and play. Architecture is unavoidable stage and play, by necessity it has to attempt to form the stage to anticipate the plays that it will carry. Strong architecture unavoidably influences the players. Long before it became a reality, the future acts of the Scottish Parliament were acted out in the imagination of the architect. As he shaped every space he would imagine it in performance and the results gave rise to patterns of space and activity. In the creation of such architecture the language that initiates a concept is slowly dispensed with and distilled down to a gesture, and that gesture becomes the physical form of the building (and that embodiment, in essence, is human.) In 1995 Miralles said to an interviewer, 'the term empathy you propose is very appropriate. I think I often work by empathy or by identification with the objects I produce. I often imagine people moving around the building, moving through walls and pillars like in the field of forces in which the occupants are an integral part of it '.[25]

For Miralles this process of distilling down to a gesture was achieved by tracing and retracing an idea over and over until it became something other than itself. In the 1995 interview, he said 'the work of repetition is very important to the production of the embodiment or of an idea, it is the longest task, for the architecture becomes recognisable beyond the specific initial data. I work with constructive, not visual criteria, and so repetition is extremely important. Each new sketch is an operation in oblivion or in the laws that are generated have an internal coherence '.[26] And the distillation of the months of thought that had formed his concept for the Parliament lay on the thirteen sheets of flimsy tracing paper he placed before Donald Dewar in the final presentation to the competition jury on 22 June 1998.[27] (The finalists had been selected on May 7th). Donald Dewar, a Labour Member of Parliament and at that time Secretary of State for Scotland, had led the cause for Scotland's relative independence, its devolution. Miralles ignored most of the elaborate models, and photomontages mounted on the walls around him, concentrating instead on a sequence of hand drawn studies he had prepared: they would give life to the essential ideas from which he would form the Parliament, and all the ideas on these flimsy sheets were to remain present in the work as it evolved and defined the essential character of the architecture as it was constructed.

By 1998 Miralles had emerged as a forceful and original architectural imagination. His Studio in Barcelona which he jointly ran with Benedetta Tagliabue, his wife and partner since the early 90's, (before that his partnership had been with his previous wife Carme Pinos). The project that had gained most attention was the Igualada Cemetery but all the work of Enric's Studio had been carefully reported in major European magazines. There were several published monographs and major exhibitions had been held in Europe, the United States and Japan. He was also as much in demand as a teacher as a practitioner: he held the Chair in Architecture at the Barcelona School, was Director of the Master Class at the Stadelschule in Frankfurt and was given the Kenzo Tange Chair at Harvard in 1992. At the time of the competition he was one of but a handful of truly original architectural imaginations world wide.

What follows is a highly detailed reading of the drawings: they are key to understanding the composer and more importantly the composition. They present a rare opportunity to enter into a creative mind. They were literally drawn out of scrapbooks. In preparing for the work he had wandered the streets of Edinburgh old and new then travelled in the company of an inspired guide the length and breadth of Scotland photographing and scribbling notes and images as he went. He was a great admirer of the Scottish people, he felt they had an affinity with his own Catalan character, and he had both studied and taught in Scotland over the years.[28]

These were the days in which all five of the finalists were presenting to the jury. On arriving Miralles thought the layout of the room was too inquisitorial so he immediately set about rearranging the furniture to give the room a more congenial atmosphere. To someone who was there, it was a surprisingly personal performance, high in drama and emotion. At certain points he would move from the sketches to pick up one of the exquisite balsa wood models which – as he fingered and described what it meant to him – became precious; he would then hand it to the jury. No one on that day could have imagined that the two principal architects of the Scottish Parliament – Miralles the builder and Dewar the politician – would be dead before construction would really begin.

There were thirteen drawings in all. Three introductory drawings established major themes and then a series of ten overlays portrayed the evolution of the idea for the Parliament in a series of orchestrations of two overarching concepts: *es un lugar mental,* the Parliament is a form in the people's mind, and *el Parliamento se reune en la Terra,* the Parliament sits in the land.

The first of the three introductory drawings is dominated by a view of the site of the Parliament from Arthur's Seat (traced from a photograph) (Illustration 1). From the hillside in the foreground he has drawn the branches of a tree whose three leaves dominate the page as they settle beside a soft tracing of the outline of the seventeenth-century mansion – Queensberry House; the decision had already been taken to restore it. The leaves suggest forms and rhythms rippling around and flowing into this place.

The texts on all the drawings are written both as instructions to himself and key thoughts. The key text attends three interlocking circles marked *A, B,* and *C*; below are the key elements: *A. Main Chamber, B. Committee Rooms, C. Public Presentations.* Below this, after commenting on the dominance of committees, he calls for 'some more dialogue between rooms', and looking at the drawing it seems that as he writes he sees an image that would be a form of dialogue. Alongside the text he draws a little cluster of leaves, the first traces of forms which eventually will become the central figures. Consider that he sees in his mind's eye the association between such spaces as leaves on a branch as he makes a tiny drawing at the conclusion of the text. The form of the leaves begins to assume larger significance as he draws, the leaves on the right dominating the page. Look closely at the drawing. At the edge of each leaf is a tiny letter *A, B* or *C*. His imagination has found in the form and spread of the leaves the figural source for the main elements of the building – the Chamber, the Committee Rooms and the place for public presentation. He writes that this sketch 'is more useful at the moment of taking formal decisions'. It seems a metaphor, and it is almost a technical statement. He explains the significance of the metaphor of the leaves:

> *the building of the parliament*
> *should sit in the place*
> *with same logic and delicacy*
> *that organises vegetal [sic] forms*
> *leaves x trees*
> *had always been an example*

Beneath that he notes 'Remember Mackintosh' reminding himself and the jury that natural forms were a driving source of inspiration for Mackintosh. His last statement: 'now the building should follow'. The implication is quite specific with this metaphorical insight the parliament will evolve.

Having offered a metaphorical vision the second sheet evokes – rather self consciously – a political vision in the three images again traced from photographs (Illustration 2). On the left a lone figure is sitting on steps which become landscape with a terse note 'the body gestures'. Below that is a lively tracing of a seated formal gathering titled 'The Highland Council meeting', between is the enigmatic statement: 'Two faces of the same attitude'. On the right of the page a careful copy of a famous photograph from the 1900's, The St Kilda Parliament, the elected leaders of the tiny and remote island of St Kilda, (revived in the cultural imagination by Douglas Dunn's 1980 novel of the same name).[29] This image has great strength for him, he writes:

> *Late XIX St Kilda Parliament*
> *To Remember this is not an archaic activity*
> *My generation (myself) has experienced that emotion*
> *Consider how different movements exist in present times*
> *Architecture should be able to talk about this*

These are offered not as nostalgic history but as a modest political ideal. These three portrayals; the individual, the Highland Council, the St Kilda Parliament he would have the architecture embrace, or in his words 'the organisation of forms should mirror this'. At the centre of the drawing he writes:

> *I imagine that a parliament building*
> *should be organic like a university campus*
> *A special kind of knowledge*
> *produces*
> *Parliament's need to have different*
> *Places where to think*
> *to talk*
> *to walk*

Across the middle of the page he holds a brief Socratic exchange: what form should it take? He replies:

> *The palace could <u>not</u> be a model*
> *The Dome should <u>not</u> be a model*

Here it must be Foster's Reichstag that was in his mind, rather than the United States Capitol. He concludes that form may lie in 'The Monastery' with its 'cloister of connections' and 'independent constructions' the emphases are Miralles. Alongside this he offers a vague drawing of the diagram for the Old College of Edinburgh University 'moving from one place to another has to have specific meaning,' he observes, 'this must not be one building but an accumulation of buildings each given distinct character, function and construction'. These are not casual observations but specific instructions for him when sees in a metaphor or mix of metaphors the gesture that will shape the stage he locks into it.

The last of the introductory drawings seems to be out of place. Visually it is more illustration than exploration. In it he refers to critical comments in the press that this foreigner was going to make the Scotland Parliament look like upturned boats (Scottish boats but on an English beach) (Illustration 3).[30] At the time of the interview the boats were not public and this drawing may have been added to the set later for exhibition.[31] Afraid people might assume that he had been tempted to shape parliament in their image, he writes:

> *I'm very happy that these boats had come in the newspapers . . .*
> *They are an image that 'illuminates' problems*
> *They are not a fast solution.*

Yet he does acknowledge the usefulness of the form:

> *The boats . . .*
> *of our first conversations*
> *come back in a natural way . . .*
> *Again they will help to decide when we*
> *Think about chambers . . .*
> *They are a wonderful example to follow*
> *Besides the more conceptual approach*

The drawings on the page are in pencil – no colour – and not as finished as the other sheets. A diagonal stream of lines crosses the page from the top left and ends in a cluster of figures – leaves in plan – but despite his protestations above they are unmistakably in the form of upturned boats.

However, the most curious figure on the page is the large drawing on the left. It is strange that so early in the design process he has such a clear image of the main chamber that he feels he must draw it. It is a significant mark, not for its boat like section, but for the extensive screened skylight the rises up behind the dais, an idea that survives into construction.

At the foot of the drawing he returns to his major preoccupation, 'The Scottish Parliament should find different building strategies according to different parts,' he continues, 'our proposal is trying to do it – it is not a single building it is an orchestrated series of constructions'.

He proceeds to ask, 'WHY NOT ONE BUILDING?' (Miralles' caps) and answers, 'A single building will have scale serious problems at the site'. Elsewhere he adds, 'Every part of the building should have the organisational form which is most coherent to its use'.

He then begins to present the set of overlays through which he will literally draw out the conceptual form of the Parliament. Layer upon layer, a palimpsested sequence of ideas from which the essential architecture will emerge. (Except for the first three layers which contain elements repeated on the later drawings, the complete series of overlays is illustrated.) Immediately he states his purpose, 'The aim of these pages . . . to remember to find the common characteristics of the site and the land and from these develop an iconography of the building of the parliament.' At the top is an abstract passage, a vague memory of Arthur's Seat. The figure flows into a most careful tracing of the west side of Reid's Close seen from above (Reid's Close is the last surviving vennel, the ancient lanes that from the earliest time bisected the mass of the ancient city). As he draws he can feel the scale and the material of the place; he notes 'granite' 'grey' and . . . 'small passages.' He adds enigmatically 'like to remember stones pile in the fields.'

On the second layer, Reid's Close from above is repeated, but now it faces a new and strange intrusion, a long amorphic object – the form of a building is emerging. Alongside he descends to ground level to offer a specific description of how he sees these undulating walls. Behind is a swiftly drawn profile of the hills. He writes, 'the new building should ... react to distant mountain profiles and reflect the changing conditions of light'. He is drawing what his mind's eye sees clearly, and as he empathises with the qualities of the place he develops a visceral sense of a material presence, 'different kinds of stone' he notes. The drawings are a fragile expression of the complex marriage of poetry, materials and utility out of which an architecture will emerge.

The third layer again repeats the trace of Reid's Close and the long undulating mass that has been formed in mind as a reflection of it. But the vignette is charged by a very precise drawing of Queensberry House, all still viewed from above. What at first seemed to be careful consideration of the actual place is instead a convenient rearrangement. This to allow the scale of Canongate to infuse his thoughts in shaping the body of the parliament – the Canongate in fact runs across the face of Queensberry House. And it is on the page that he realises that the restoration of this seventeenth century mansion will as he notes 'add scale and precision to the project'. He explores this by imagining the view from within the old house of the new Parliament, an exact drawing, a view from a window. 'It is the same building,' he writes, '... fragment of the city, real scale, the buildings he notes like neighbours, <u>not</u> monumental' (his emphasis).

Fourth, has Queensberry House traced again in softest outline. Here his interest is in the walls and gates that once enclosed a formal garden (Illustration 4). On the left he created an imaginary garden from the evidence of a few surviving engravings. 'In between the walls,' he writes, 'it is possible to dream ... a resting place'. He colours the garden as an eighteenth-century formal garden and allows wistful lines of desire to flow from the site into the park. At this stage in his thinking the surviving and restored historical buildings are allowed to frame the new work.

At the fifth level what was a void in the view of Queensberry house in the fourth becomes a garden riotously in bloom (Illustration 5). He is captivated by the noble presence the house will give to the Parliament, captivated by recreating a magic garden at the centre. He draws as he was sketching from life on a spring morning. The house, a wispy outline in the distance; the garden a patchwork of plantings and forms, 'The cloister garden,' he writes, 'should reflect the personality of parliament.' Though not noted on the drawings those around him remember his brief enthusiasm for matching the colour of the flowers to colours of the political parties, (carefully planted, one would assume, in proportion to party representation and subject to fluctuations in political fortune). He was dreaming of a garden formed from a salad of Scottish landscapes in miniature, '. . . a structured pattern coming from land cultivation'. Though as the plans evolved and the Parliament grew larger, the garden is one of the few themes present at the beginning that does not evolve. The garden was evidence of the early desire for a compounding of reality at the centre that finally results in the spectacular invention of the Members' Foyer.

Layer six has a deliberate and powerful character. The Canongate has gone – it has served its purpose as a register (Illustration 6). Now the complete and careful drawing of Queensberry House is flanked on either side with long figures formed from undulating masses. Starting in the upper left and thrusting diagonally across the page a swath of green ends in a concentrated knuckle alongside.

The drawing illustrates not a probable reality but a conceptual dilemma – by what gesture can the spirit of the natural landscape, flowing from the park, be driven into the Parliament. The force of the stream of landscape makes the suggested figure round Queensberry House tentative and stoic. At the end of this muscle of landscape he writes, 'This construction', referring to the abstract passage of land, 'answers some of the questions . . . The building sits on the land, The people sit on the land' the land and the people and the parliament are one.[32] Below that he writes:

> *The Scottish Parliament!*
> *The scale of it*
> *individual*
> *human*
> *independent.*

The relation between text and image reinforces the meaning; here is a cry from the heart. On the right of the page he writes, 'from now on we need to be more abstract'. And then explains, perhaps to himself, 'give a more technical definition'. The last words on the page, '(The previous page is not ashamed of this one)', the parenthesis is his.

True to his word the final four pages move out of the descriptive into a thrilling display of his first attempts to spatialise the concept. Remember what is being explored is a possible condition of experienced reality. Structure and accommodation are never absent but they are subservient to this need to reveal, to distil significant form from the essence of the context. His actions are laying the basis for discovering a landscape unique to this place.

By the seventh layer a man and a woman sit on the passage of land that flows across the page but here it lands directly in the centre of the complex (Illustration 7). Gone are Queensberry House and the tentative structures that flanked it and in their place the landform flows into an extraordinary figure, red, awkward, almost the pulsating heart of parliament.

On close inspection it is an assembly chamber and tiny figures crowd the terraces. He writes, 'the parliament belongs to the land'. And as he draws he finds both confirmation and deep satisfaction in what he has drawn, he writes:

> *It was the idea expressed on these pages that gave a way to follow*
> *Seating together*
> *Seating together at different scales*
> *Seating at the land*

On the corner of this sheet Miralles feels the need to reveal something of his creative process he adds:

> *Note; you have a word:*
> *EMBODIEMENT* [sic]
> *that we [do] not have*
> *It explains:*
> *this identification through body*
> *gesture*
> *Understood through body.*

As he draws and imagines this place, his being is consumed by it, he mimes it with gesture and movement, he wills its presence out of his own physicality. 'It is crucial to meditate on the iconography of our parliament,' he writes, and these little drawings are explicit products of his meditation, the drawing carries content that has no words.

This is a work shaped to survive the centuries, to assume layers of meaning from the political centre of the nation; its nature, its appropriateness, its significance as architecture is formed on these pages. He steps aside from the conceptual narrative on this page and offers editorial note, on the public character of the parliament. He notes, alongside a little drawing of fish in a bowl that 'glass isolates ... it [creates] a kind of fishbowl.' Presumably, he again has the German Reichstag in mind where Foster assembled the German parliament beneath a glass dome open to the sky and overlooked by a generous public processional and gallery. For Miralles, political debate should not be merely a public spectacle. The main chamber must hold and enhance a 'concentration of speech'. He was wholly in support of the requirement that the new Parliament support and enhance the transactions of the lawmakers, but that the public dissemination of their deliberations depends not on the architecture of the building but on the most ambitious use of electronic media, from the simple access through television to personal engagement available to every citizen through the interactivity of the web.

The eighth level is a beautiful and elegiac drawing; all the elements of the composition are becoming clear to him (Illustration 8). It shows how effortlessly this intersection of ideas can be held in balance. The drawing implies once again a landscape sweeping across the page but forward movement is blocked by parliament and comes to a staggering stop, folding and buckling space beneath a winged structure. The flash of the green landform and the winged structure in blue are flanked by a passage of water formed from the echoes of this disturbance. Though abstracted, it is again a tracing of the site seen from above but only the essential forces are represented. The discreet numbers mark the salient edges of this fantasy. '1, 2, 3' are explained in a tiny note: '1' the slashing passage of green is the *land*, '2' the agitated patch of blue is *water*, and '3' the complex folded structure is the *air*. And at the point where, in the future, the main chamber will evolve, they suggest a complex fusion.

Though abstract in effect they are tangible elements in the

formation of architecture. From past experience Miralles knew how to take such slender gestures of forces in harmony and evolve them into a concrete material reality. Here is evidence of the limits of language in the composition of new reality, forcing the landscape to play out in his imagination allowing him to conceive of this turbulent conclusion in a folded translucent plane, as is held in check, beneath a great glass roof. In his imagination he has placed himself standing high above this place when he writes: 'We will talk about a Public Concourse/ MSP Concourse ... A gallery covering and crossing where the geography of Scotland could be shown, A Gallery of Maps.'

The ninth layer is a less certain more reflective coda; maybe a response to the appearance of water on eight (Illustration 9). On eight this force field, act of nature has a completeness only when all elements are present so water has to find its place in the landscape and the River Trumble re-emerges. The Trumble was a little river lost to history which once flowed on or near this place. (Not totally lost, the presence of the Parliament has discovered it in a culvert beneath the site and it manages to find its way into the Firth of Forth). Miralles again offers the bird's-eye view of the site tracing all the surrounding buildings on the Canongate but here extending the view out to the buildings of the Palace. The actual site is empty save for the wraith of green and the pools carried over from the previous drawing. On the left he carefully represents the course of the Trumble from an early map of the city. The site is strangely empty and silent, as if waiting for the river to re-emerge and finds its level. On the map the river flows out of the Canongate passing by the place now covered by the Parliament. There may once have been a loch here and this teases his imagination to represent the outbuildings to the palace reflected in a sheet of water. This is not archaeology but a conceptual need to make all the elements of nature surround and define the place. He seeks the essence, 'The Old

Edinburgh in its hostile environment was indeed symbolic of all lowland Scotland the surface of which was pitted with meres and lochans.'

The tenth and final layer begins with the note 'this page is not a final page – just the overlapping of previous ones. The parliament should have the same intensity in all parts, different but not unbalanced,' (Illustration 10). And as if to confirm this the upturned boats and the view from Arthur's Seat reappear. The Trumble is retraced but fades into insignificance in the margins of the glorious recollection of all that has gone before. Here all concepts come together to form a new reality for Parliament. The sweeping landform leads the forces of nature into the site from the south to be met and held by the resolute bulk of Queensberry House. The collision produces an explosive effect, bubbling space into a series of massive volumes (still reminiscent of leaves and upturned boats) dominated by the great chamber for the new Scottish Parliament. The drawing vibrates with the intensity of the engagement and the space between Parliament and the old house is consumed by a soaring warped plane, transparent as the air. A parliament formed out of the resolution between the land and the city between nature and history between the past and future. He ends with a command:

> *To balance*
> *land and city*
> *at the Parliament Building*
> *the iconography should come out of that . . .*

Miralles ended by giving each of the jury the gift of a little flip book formed from the reduction of the sketches that let them play with the image of the building emerging from the slopes of Holyrood Park. They were enthralled.

All these forces were kept in play as the design progressed, however for many months the space between the cluster of towers around the Chamber and Queensberry House, despite numerous studies, continually failed to find a form to match the conceptual flourish of the conceptual drawings.

Many of the same elements appear in the formal presentations yet they seem more diffuse and distant than in the sketches. However, some of the texts add clarity. 'The parliament,' he writes, 'should define the end of the Canongate as more than just a construction along a street.' It must 'reinforce the existing qualities of the place'. To the idea of the parliament sitting on the land he adds 'This is a way of marking the conceptual distance from Holyrood Palace. Whereas the Palace is a building situated on the landscape ... the new Scottish Parliament would sit within the land. ... Instead of an overwhelming monument which only relates to dimensions and rhetorical forms.' He asked himself and the jury 'How is it going to be FUNDAMENTALLY DISTINCTIVE from other parliaments?' The answer is in the drawings.

His was a mature creative mind highly aware of how he composed. From the *El Croquis* interview in 1995 he said 'I'm not interested at all in allusive reality, the connections are made backwards in time, or towards history, or forwards towards a utopia; or towards a given paradigm or language ... what interests me more is a sort of incorporation of infinite integration ...'

On 7 July 1998 the commission to design the Scottish Parliament was awarded to EMTB/RMJM. EMBT are the initials Enric Miralles and Benedetta Tagliabue (his partner and wife) RMJM is a venerable Scottish based international practice named after its founders Robert Matthew and Stirrat Johnson-Marshall and Partners. Eric Miralles' close collaborator in RMJM was Mick Duncan, who with his Managing Director Brian Stewart has been central to the creative process in ensuring that all the opaque originality of the Miralles drawings was preserved in every element of the new Parliament.[33]

All the conceptual and compositional elements that were present in the winning submission would be under continuous and subtle transformation between the award of the commission in 1998 and the completion of the final approved design in June of 2000. The brief expanded with the ambitions of the client yet the conceptual structure held and evolved. The only part of the complex completely designed in May 1999 was the wing for the Members of the Scottish Parliament (MSP). They occupy a disciplined block running at a right angle to the Canongate on the west side of Queensberry House. Miralles sought to 'convey the sense of the building as a series of individuals. The Parliament should not have the appearance of an office building' he declared. Each MSP has a vaulted cell which on every floor enters on one side into a grand corridor 'the main communication room – conversations in passing – comments'. And on the other there are 'individual windows which become seating balconies'. These seating balconies are an original and powerful architectural invention. Each cell has a projected bay on the west wall, exactly in the form of a seat, all slightly different, a seat in which each parliamentarian is alone yet surrounded by the city and the landscape. Inside, the window seat and the flowing forms embossed in the vault ceiling cause an intriguing disturbance to each office. Outside, the combined mass of window seats creates a dense vertical landscape, a three dimensional tapestry ordered in the mass yet infinitely varied in the detail. The idea was encouraged in Miralles' imagination by the way the John Knox House juts out of alignment giving a subtle game of cross views and political implications.[34] (There is the presence of another Scottish personage in their making; Miralles was fond of Sir Henry Raeburn's painting of the *Reverend Robert Walker Skating on Duddingston Loch* and there may be a hint of his profile in the profile of the bays).

These broad corridors were conceived as a space carved out of a solid, and a vault brings light and air from the east into each MSP cell. The east face of the wing is as original as the clustering of window seats in the west, with ventilation sockets cut back to the line of the cell vaults assisting cross ventilation, windows lost behind oak screens and a quirky geometric pattern of drainage hoppers and gutters in stainless steel carrying rainwater, which criss-crosses diagonally down the façade.[35] Yet to be heard, but much anticipated, will be the harmonies produced by the cascades of water in the heavy rains of Edinburgh. Such invention, far from being indulgent, is the product of a vision that would use this element to create a metaphorical representation of unity and difference in the community of the MSPs. The MSP suite is one of the four formative stages that combine to shape the play of the parliament. Miralles wrote, 'I characterise this building as a series of individuals. This place is consciously shaped by the body'. He engaged in a form of predictive stage management as he would mentally move with the MSPs out of the building onto the courtyard, 'it is not difficult to imagine,' he wrote, 'pensive thoughts outside the building with thoughts running through the mind – seeking the help of a reflective walk during a pensive situation'.

While the final form of the Chamber remained undecided at the May 1999 presentation, the space it would sit on, the Main Hall, was complete. In all its wayward detail it seems both to support and even threaten the Chamber above. Miralles anticipated that the Main Hall 'will have a very strong impact on the Public's view of the Parliament'. It is formed beneath long vaults whose surface is incised with a meandering scatter of huge St Andrews crosses. There are generous curving cuts through the vaults letting light into the public passage and scarping the underside of the great hall above. Miralles wrote, 'the vaulted space is lit by deep light wells where many different light conditions occur, east light, evening light and direct views to the nearby hills'. The room, however, feels subterranean, yet it does possess *an ancient archaic feeling*. The entry passes under a slender extensive canopy that is shaped as a *non monument* – it is as if the skin of the Parliament had been pulled out to embrace the public. The result is an effect in which the Chamber rests on the people rather than in the land; a strange and visceral connection between the people and the politician, a kind of dependency, one upon the other.

After May of 1999 the complex cluster of leaf-shaped volumes housing everything from the Chamber and the committees to the administration and the press remained confused and unresolved as they jostled to find coherence both in function and effect. Miralles and the architects plunged into months of adjusting and readjusting the arc of members seating to find the form that would most effectively support the debate in the Parliament. Physically, operationally and in the public imagination the Scottish Parliament was expected to be radically different from both Westminster and the Capitol in Washington. By plan, debate in the Scottish Chamber would have neither the oppositional structure that so marks British parliamentary behaviour nor the imperial semicircle that forces the US senate to sit at the pleasure of the Vice President. He knew what had to be found:

> *For the quality of the debate*
> *It is important that not only the*
> *MSP's could embrace each other, but also*
> *The Room should embrace them*

As the design developed, the curve of seating became overextended and the ends were folded in to form an awkward termination. It was far from the effect he sought. In a document prepared in May of 1999 *Scottish Parliamentary Explanatory Document*, Miralles' conceptual inspiration for the form of the Chamber and the Committee Rooms was never more explicit: a cluster of slender branches run diagonally across the page to the three leaves, the largest exactly where the Parliament would gather (it is the same image that he had used in the presentation to the Jury). His notes on the page state that he seeks 'an equilibrium and richness between the rooms and the users. I do not imagine a parliament dominated by either a cupola or a debating chamber beneath it'. At this time the debating chamber found its appropriate form (one much present in Miralles' earlier work) an arch: though, in plan shaped from an arc and two tangents; a tense curve which would bring all members in contact one with another. This tense curve resolved the major concern for the politicians that the ends of the hall were too far from the middle; that those unfortunate enough to be so seated would somehow be at a disadvantage – too far from the centre to be noticed. When the new arrangement was laid over the rectangular formalities of the Parliament's temporary quarters in the Assembly Hall of the Church of Scotland, the politicians quickly noticed the obvious difference that in the new Chamber they would never be physically in opposition to one another. It was also clearly a form able to accommodate whatever mix of (currently seven) political parties were elected to serve Scotland (a rainbow parliament as David McCrone has called it). The same search for individuality marked the shaping of the committee rooms. Each capped by soaring vaults that are carved into and burst with light; Miralles was deliberate 'Each are individual rooms, not one more of a series'.

Though much was becoming firm, the penetration of the landscape into the heart of the complex had yet to find its form. For a brief period the development drawings began to lose their conceptual force; missing was that climactic point – suggested in the conceptual sketch – a rippling field of energy at the centre.

Between mid-November 1999 and the beginning of February 2000, the brief expanded and demanded more space, while at the same time Historic Scotland requested that the project cause less disruption to the interior of Queensberry House.[36] In February/March of 2000 these pressures led to the most brilliant amendment to the design – the creation of a Garden Lobby. The previous plans for Parliament had carved open the street level of the old house to create a passage linking the MSP wing to the Chamber. The solution was to restore the rooms on the ground floor of Queensberry House and build the connecting passage into the garden. Pure serendipity – the demand to create a structure in the garden – gave a context within which Miralles was able to produce the conceptual climax to the intersection of land and air promised in the drawings; the resolution of the penetration of the park and the Crags into the heart of the complex.

In his first drawing from February/March 2000, Miralles sees a dense canopy of leaf forms – precisely drawn – to cover the space, this would evolve into an undulating sequence of arched metal structures carrying generous skylights and creating an astonishing space. There is one fragile drawing of this complex, it shows a three-dimensional swarm of structures; it is drawn effortlessly, almost casually with the radii and tangents set out with such precision that it would translate unaltered into the extraordinary structure that has resulted. This is a wholly original construction of space whose effect will be as much psychological as visual. It becomes the restless dynamic heart of the political community and continually changing in the light. It is ambiguous, open to endless interpretation, an infinitely shifting experience both of the stage and the players, never predictable or easy to know. As the idea crystallised he was concerned with the loss of the garden and considered having a passage of grass roll in from the park and rise up and over the foyer, but this did not happen. The final resolution allows the lawmakers to move from the Garden Lobby into the sheltered garden beneath the cascading face of the MSP wing, which flows into the rib of landform that follows the path of the earliest drawing into Holyrood Park.

Early in 2000 Miralles was diagnosed with a tumour in his brain. All was done to help and on the advice of friends he went to Texas for treatment. From his hospital bed in Houston, Miralles faxed the team in Edinburgh expressing happiness both with the final project as it was presented and with all those who had worked with him.

Transcript of the fax from Enric Miralles, Houston, 28 March 2000:

> *John [Gibbons], Mick [Duncan], Brian [Stewart] (The architects first)* [sic]
>
> *A picturesque doctor will operate me on Wednesday but I will send a note for the debate.*
> *I like them to read if I'm not*
> *there.*
> *Maybe is not very Scottish!*
>
> *A project, the making of a project is a learning process.*
> *To learn to be together.*
> *The kindness of each other*
> *or to hear from*
> *each other ...*
> *For that reason the newspaper cartoons*
> *are excellent.*

"The Spanish man selling ice cream to the beach ..."
but this is not the reality.
A very good group of people closed is EMBT
RMJM
And I think we have been doing an excellent job,
listening,
adapting ...
We have created a piece of
Scotland.
The way the building merges the history with the landscape is
very good.
We are in the middle point.
The project is ready
(Could be cheaper,
 a bit smaller ...)
but the project is ready.
do not be afraid.
Scots never are (or so they said)
I hope to be able to see you at the debate
And open the building together if
God allows.
The team will help overcome
We are in contact.
I like to say something.
The lobby
is a fantastic piece ...
is the only way. Queensberry is not
an isolated object.
The heart

of the complex and give
energy . . . offering
a listening chamber
to be like a lamp in to
the scotch landscape.

Final Design Approval was given on 20 June 2000, and two weeks later on 3 July 2000 Enric Miralles died. Work had to proceed, yet the loss was enormous. Designing in detail continued after his death both Edinburgh and Barcelona committed to preserving every element of the design.

The Parliament exists in the fusion between the topography of the Park and the structure of the City, embedded in the geological and social history of the place. Its form neither a preconceived portrait nor representation but drawn out of the physical residue of the place and the multiple performances of Parliament. This Parliament is an assembly of parts, informal, decentralised; an inhabited landscape metaphorically embodying the culture of Scotland. The individual and the collective brought together in metaphorical landscape, landform straining to echo the physical and the cultural landscape of Scotland. This set of conceptual instructions results in a work of architecture which is informal, internally directed, introverted on the ground yet drawing in the sky. It is ahistorical, unfashionable, unstylish, and wholly original. The result is a sequence of stages imbued with quiet dramas and mysteries which will insinuate themselves into the imaginations of those who come to form the future of the nation.

The Parliament is a wholly new and untried instrument which has the promise of magnifying and harmonising the desires of the nation. Its marvellous promise is given life for me in the Louis MacNeice poem 'The Autumn Journal':

What is it we want really?
For what end and how
If it is something feasible obtainable
Let us dream it now
And pray for a possible land
Not of sleep walkers, not of angry puppets [?]
But where both heart and brain can understand
The monuments of our fellows
Where life is a choice of instruments and none
Is debarred his natural music . . . [37]

The new Parliament itself is an instrument formed out of the culture, the city and the land, and a wholly original instrument, never before played, with a capacity for making the national music that demands imagination.

On 11 October 2000 Donald Dewar died at the Western General Hospital in Edinburgh, as the result of a brain haemorrhage. In April 2000, he had been diagnosed with heart problems and, in May, underwent surgery to replace a leaking heart valve, (he was still recovering when he heard of Miralles death).

As he stood on the scaffold facing death in 1677, the Covenanter martyr James Renwick declared, 'There is a great storm coming which shall try your foundations, Scotland must be rid of Scotland before the deliverance comes.' Devolution has rediscovered Renwick and the bitter irony in his words is seen as a challenge to all who believe in the promise of self government.

The Drawings

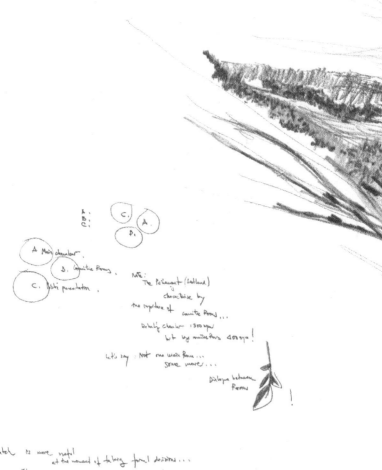

A :
B :
C :

A Main chamber.

B. Committee Rooms.

C. Public presentation.

NOTE :
The Parliament (Scotland) is
characterise by
the importance of committee Rooms...

Debating chamber 1300 sqm
but by committee Rooms 4000 sqm !

Let's say : Not one main Room...
Some more....

Dialogue between
Rooms

!

has stated as more useful
at the moment of taking formal decisions...

It seems a metaphore and it is almost a
technical statement...

The building of the parliament
should seat in the place
with the same logic & delicacy
that organize vegetal forms...

Leaves & trees had always been an example ...

Remember Mackintosh ...

Now the building should follow

Illustration 1

I imagine that a Parliament building
should be expressed
as a university campus...
A special kind of
practices...
Parliamentarians need to
places where to think,
to talk,
to walk...

The Palace could *not* be the model.
The Dome should *not* be the model.
The Monastery...
Cluster of connected
independent

The "body politic"...

Two faces of the same attitude.

Highland Council meeting 1986

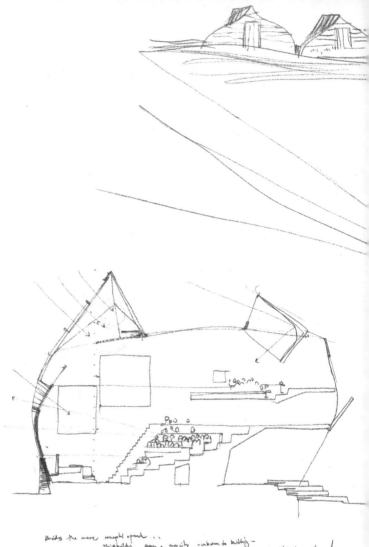

Besides the more sculptural approach...

Shipbuilding poses a capacity —unknown to building—
to prefabricate fragments with a very high finishing quality. !

The Scottish Parliament
stockpile different building strategies assigning to different parts. (look slides)
Our proposal is trying to do it ... it a
It is an orchestrated semi

the books
now for the conversation
come back in a useful way...

they will help to decide when who
think about alumino...

They are a wonderful example to follow.

I'm very happy that these book had come to the newspapers...
They are an image that "illuminates" the
problem ... They are not a fast motion.

how to Barr
Monument,

If is possible that drawings to feel
the material reality of inner space...
Let's look to some schematic models.
And some old photographs,

bildg
fraction.... WHY ONE BUILDING?   A single bildg will have scale serious problems at tw site.

Illustration 3

walls . . .
enclose gardens .
hedges . . . . .

Builds
Enters a imaginative
material
that w
(au

A between walls
is possible to dream
about an exciting place . . .
place to rest.

Some walls . . . enclosure
there is in there . . .
They do not need to be Rebuild,
The gardens in its vitality
keeps everything alive !

I Remember Extrall Called (August.)

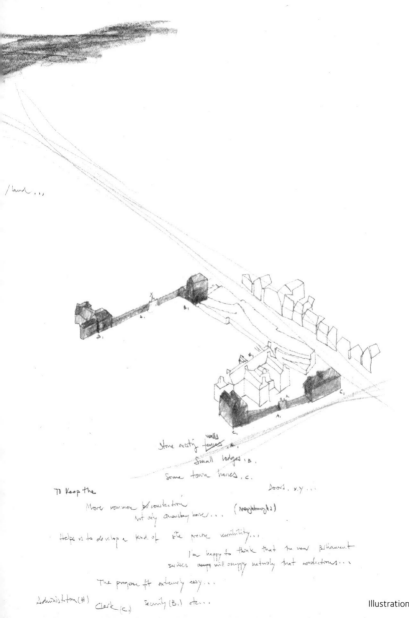

Illustration 4

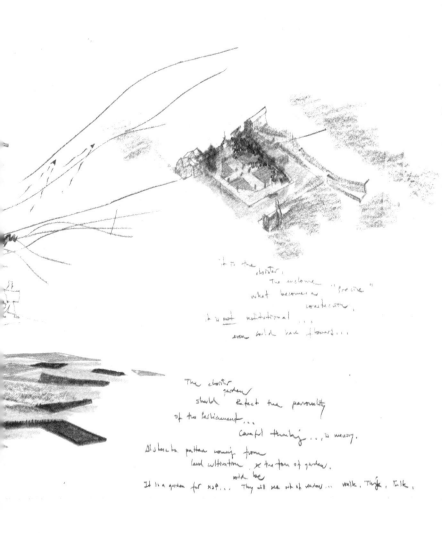

It is the
cloister,
The enclosure. "precise"
what becomes an
architecture.
it is not institutional ...
even hold back flowers...

The cloister
garden
should Reflect the personality
of the Parliament ...
Careful thinking ... is messy.

Abstract pattern coming from
land cultivation ... the form of garden.
with bee
It is a garden for use ... They will see out of windows ... walk, Think, Talk.

Illustration 5

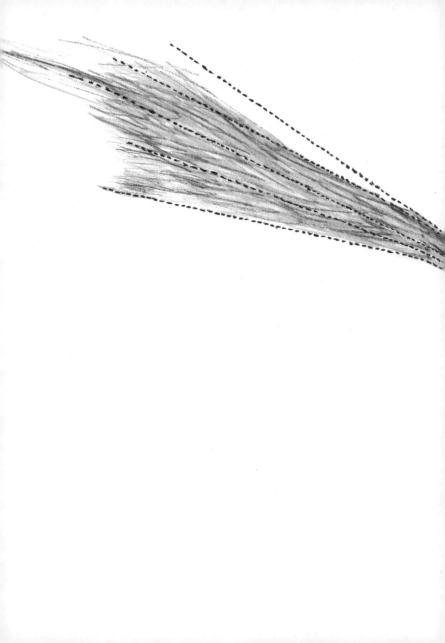

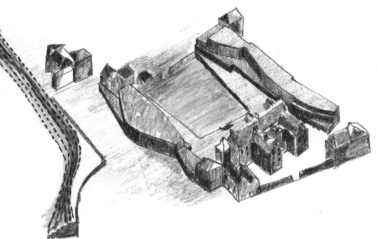

This conclusion...
answers some of the
questions...
The building sits in the land,
People sits in the land,

The scottish parliament !

The scale of it...

individual,
human
independent...

The Monastery
+ the land.

Illustration 6

It is curious to meditate about
iconography of new parliament...

Literal ~~transparency = glass~~

It is inspiring...
glass isolates
it = kind
of

TV, Radio.
The Parliament debates
are followed at home or at the car.

at views, newspapers...

The Parliament needs concentration on speech...

After our first conversation
we were very afraid of

to learn

It was the idea express in these page

Note: If You have a word:
EMBODIMENT
that we not have

An explained
this identification thigh body
gesture...

understand thigh body...

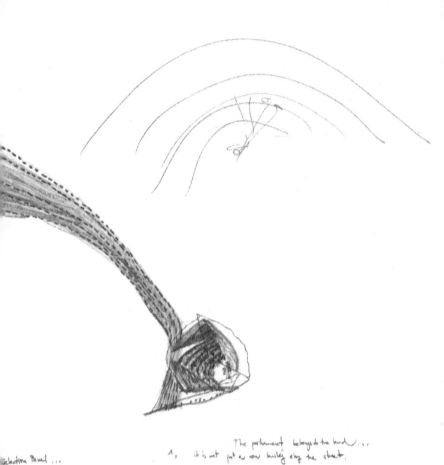

The parliament belongs to the land ...
it is not just a new building along the street.

Selection Panel ...

... important to do modulates,
to use
to Develop necessity ...
easy to follow working ...

Seating together
Seating together at different scales ...

... at the land ...

Illustration 7

1. band .
2. water .
3. Air .

We will talk about Public someone / MST tomorrow . . .

A gallery among a many where the geography of scotland address someone .

(A kind of "gallery of Maps".) .

Illustration 8

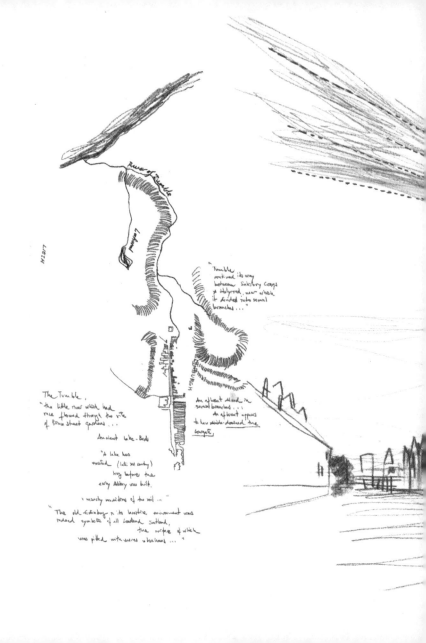

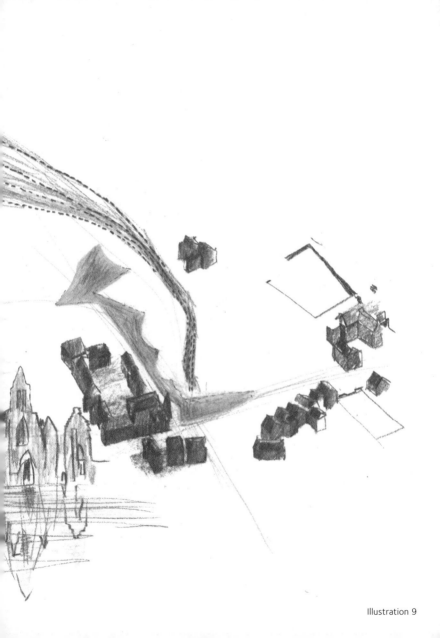

Illustration 9

Illustration 10

Wisdom, Justice, Compassion, Integrity

At the Opening Ceremony of the Scottish Parliament, 1 July 1999, Donald Dewar spoke on behalf of the people of Scotland, thanking the Queen for presenting the Mace of Scotland to the Parliament, inscribed on the Mace were the words Wisdom, Justice, Compassion, Integrity. Some of what he said:

> *This is about more than our politics and our laws. This is about who we are, how we carry ourselves. In the quiet moments today, we might hear some echoes from the past:*
>
> *The shout of the welder in the din of the great Clyde shipyards:*
> *The speech of the Mearns, with its soul in the land;*
> *The discourse of the enlightenment, when Edinburgh and Glasgow were a light held to the intellectual life of Europe;*
> *The wild cry of the Great Pipes;*
> *And back to the distant cries of the battles of Bruce and Wallace.*
>
> *Wisdom, Justice. Compassion, Integrity. Timeless values.*
> *Honourable aspirations for this new forum of democracy,*
> *born on the cusp of a new century.*

*We are fallible. We will make mistakes. But we will never lose
sight of what brought us here: the striving to do right by the
people of Scotland; to respect their priorities; to better their lot;
and to contribute to the commonweal.*

*I look forward to the days ahead when this Chamber will sound
with debate, argument and passion when men and women from all
over Scotland will meet to work together for a future built from the
first principles of social justice.*

In Performance

The politics of the Miralles imagination has made this Parliament an
informal, restless place, seeking an experience of continual change (his
realities like his personality could not abide being bored), anti-authority,
continually open to new ideas and possibilities. It confounds expectations,
it makes no predictions, suffers no illusion. It is architecture as landscape,
not portrait – it is not readable in stylistic ways, it has no word traces of
classical or medieval figures; even the simplicities of modernism cannot
explain what is going on here. This is a thing shaped by the poetic
manipulation of the circumstances of its context and its construction.

The forms are new and strange; the complexity results from being
formed as if out of nature, allowing free and informal association of
the parts and plays. It appears ambiguous because nothing like it has
been seen before, this unfamiliarity and originality is a gift to Scotland's
imagination. (Apart from the work of Mackintosh, I cannot think of any
other work in Scotland's modern history, which could be so described).
How does one approach something utterly new and different yet embedded
in the past? The question would have pleased both Miralles and Donald
Dewar because, and with more profound consequences, the same must be

asked of the new Parliament, and in both cases the answer will only emerge in time and through use. Not yet knowing or having experience with the nature of the place; not wishing to disturb in any obvious way the emerging character of the new parliamentary culture, it must be acknowledged that this is a place designed to have influence in ways ambiguous but not wholly unpredictable. The architecture does not impose, does not give marching orders, rather it weaves surprising patterns of movements in space, a spatial dance that will orchestrate the toing and froing in an MSP's day.

Miralles felt a close connection between Scotland and Catalonia: they both shared a history of external threats and domination, and a suppression of language (in Scotland it was merely the embarrassment of sounding too Scottish). Overly romanticised perhaps but leading him to believe he was uniquely able to conceptualise a parliament for Scotland. As an outsider his imagination was free from the inhibitions and anxieties that had stunted the Scottish imagination in the twentieth century. Beginning with the Adams family and the making of classical Edinburgh, through the creation of the mercantile palaces of Glasgow and ending in the work of the brilliant and forlorn Charles Rennie Mackintosh, Scottish architecture in the eighteenth and nineteenth centuries had a creative ambition that at times had an influence across Europe, yet failed to develop in the twentieth. It was a failure not of talent but of patronage: the wealth and wish for prestige of the landowners, the industrialists and the nobility had either gone or gone south.

A century in whose beginnings Scottish creativity was immortalised in the architecture and art of Mackintosh,[38] ended with the Mackintosh legacy revived in the ambitions of the Miralles Parliament.[39] Miralles was more ambitious for Scotland than most Scots were capable of or would dare. Miralles was struck by the parallels between the work of Mackintosh and Gaudi.[40] What must be asked is why Scotland was unable to learn from Mackintosh as Catalonia learned from Gaudi, but there may be still time.

Though he has no equivalent, Miralles can be compared to others in the avant-garde. His methods and derivation of form from nature, context, and even (by his own admission) from the work of such as Le Corbusier and Louis Kahn, placed him in the wide and confused field of activity, loosely grouped under the title post-modernism. Architects theorising from science and literary theory, from post-structuralism and deconstructionist critical procedures, have produced works that look superficially similar, yet he is as different from them as they from one another. Each pursues highly singular visions, distinct strategies to shape the experiences of space and reality. Miralles' work is sensual and collagist in contrast to the strategic and rational procedures of the many he could be compared with.[41] His work can certainly be described as modern Baroque – the attention to human circumstances and the constructional basis for many of his details – as well as being infused with a sense of humour. It also contains some of the elements that marked the modernism of Gaudi: a concern for total design, fluidity of space (especially in the use of the double façade and continuity of line), definition of aggregated elements, even constructed elements as the basis of ornamentation, the use of ornamentation independent of the architectural structure but often symbolic of structure.[42] Although it may seem obvious, it must be remembered that the work carries such characteristics because they were intentionally present in the architect's mind from the very beginning: he was composing in relation to achieving such effects.

It must be accepted that Miralles often seems to have created compositional and spatial problems in order to demonstrate how he could solve them: the tortuous path of the stair that takes the public into the Chamber, the turbulent structure of the roof of the Garden Lobby and above all the compound structures that carry the great beamed ceiling of the Chamber, all eschew structural economy, not only for decoration but for spatial effect.

The Parliament has had so little time to speak. Consider its strange strength and silence as the simplest response to there being, as yet, nothing to say except the physical sense of it having emerged out of the land and the history of this place. How does one talk about such work? When architecture was made from a set of approved elements all with words, named parts, and predictive effects, the task of the critic was to assess comparatively how this composition of familiar parts measured up to the benchmarks of quality (Beethoven or the brothers Adam). This process was as true in judging Modernism as it was for High Classicism. The collapse of faith in the dogmas of Modernism created a confused freedom, giving rise to much that was ill-conceived, some that was powerful and all relatively inexplicable, offering no easy comparisons either for understanding or judging. There are commonalities in the nature of creativity among the arts, all seek to give form to human experience; all are equally concerned with capturing through their different media human feeling and qualities, gesture, mood, colour tone; all can be regarded both in their production and their effect as extensions of the body. Such an attitude gives the firmest and most generous apparatus for approaching a new work, allow the spatial harmonies – visual music – to engage and entertain the senses. Surrender the imagination to the forms and spaces, not looking for familiar objects and places with names. What follows is an exploration of and a projection into the composition of the new Parliament. It seeks to uncover ways of understanding and enjoying the work. It offers an examination of the work in its own terms without reference to precedence; a willingness to begin the process of exploration of a work by surrendering to its performance without intellectualising or questioning.

The new Parliament treats the politician with the utmost respect, much more some may feel, than they deserve. (To adapt a very Scottish observation: *She canna be any good as an MSP a' kent her brither*.) But keep in mind that this is a work for the long haul, a projection into an unforeseeable future. Consider the three major parts coming together to provide a daily symphonic experience for the Members. The first movement is in the slow orderly adagio of the MSP Building, the second in the tempestuous scherzo of the Garden Lobby, leading in the grand finale to the quiet crescendo of the Chamber.

Each MSP, in his or her own way, will have to learn to wear the constraints and flourishes of the cell-like offices. Tolerating the gaze of colleagues passing – nowhere to hide. Will the window seats be used and if used what effect will they have? Each member may be briefly alone in the window but cannot escape the passing gaze of his or her colleagues gathering and gossiping, plotting and planning in the wide passage that unites all the offices. Imagine a quiet moment when it seems appropriate to experiment with the seat in the window, and just as it begins to feel right, somebody knocks on the door and gives thumbs-up. (Miralles sought here as elsewhere to achieve an affect of openness, of being accessible; it was the MSPs who requested that their offices be screened, if desired, from the corridor.) As in the Chamber, the allocation of the offices will require the greatest delicacy in balancing relationships, between parties, between seniorities and between enemies. Conversation and arguments and ideas that germinate in the broad corridors of the MSP wing will be carried down the elevator into the heart of the community, into the Garden Lobby.

The Garden Lobby: the promise Miralles made to the jury to give form to a climactic event at the heart of the composition produced this heroic stage, a structure of compelling vigour.

> *Thirteen leaf-shaped roof lights are inserted into the curved plane,*
> *all of different sizes and orientations nestling together as if caught*
> *in the eddies of a stream. The building edge zigzags with the roofs*
> *to interlock garden and space together. The leaf forms are defined*
> *by tubular steel beams between which lie bow trusses of laminated*
> *oak braced crosswise and lengthwise by steel rods, creating a space*
> *that is brilliantly lit; that seems gregarious even when there is*
> *nobody there.*[43]

This is the structuring of experience above function, as are the carved columns on which it rests, ever in a still motion, still music, and of course highly functional beyond utility, (the nineteenth century would have called it decorated construction). The restless churning waves of wood and steel, stimulating the informal desires between individuals and agendas and party politics. ('Am I up to this place?' she wonders). This is a strong, strange place which will long have influence on generations of use; a provocative view into the future. Nothing like it exists anywhere. Conversations drift through the screen of wall onto the edge of the landscape that leads to the Park. We do behave differently in the wilds than in the midst of a city. Sometimes on a hillside there is the temptation to skip, hop and dance in the freedom of the place. Cities can also be so tempting but the dance is different. This is a joyous, restless space bathed in light, filling, imbuing all with its energy, demanding courage from all who gather there.

From the Garden Lobby an elegant and formal staircase rises to the Chamber, but it also connects to the sequence of short towers that house the committee rooms, the leaf shaped volumes that jostled about the centre from first concept drawings. There are four towers and the wall onto the Canongate which rise out of the ground, each in plan part leaf, part boat, a blunt stern and a sharp cantilevered prow. They fan out sweetly between and Chamber and the garden, the highest at the centre.[44] These are the engines of the new Parliament where all legislation is formulated and prepared for debate. In form they vary, but at their most developed Miralles shaped a series of distinct spaces in which the committees would gather beneath vast warped ceilings, twisted upward to bring light to the deliberations. Forceful forms to encourage people to think no small thoughts!

While the Garden Lobby produces a confusion of people and activities, eating and drinking and browsing and laughing all in continual ebb and flow of combination and disassociation, it is in total contrast to the ordered community they become in the Chamber; everything in the nature and material of the place enhancing the pure pleasure in human engagement. From the Committee Rooms the members move on into the Chamber along a glass-enclosed passage suspended from the roof beams of the hall; a highly formal passage that gives a sense of purification to the procession into the Chamber. This stage is set to support both the unity of the parliamentary community and the intimate association of ideas among individuals. Members' desks in an ellipse, held in balance, at rest, gathered beneath the spans of a vast timber and steel roof structure, an echo of the stepped beam roof that still rests over the place of the earliest house of parliament. It is a noble space, warmed by oak and sycamore panelling that fully encases the walls and bathed in as much broad daylight as Scotland allows. A slight illusion as the natural is enhanced by discreetly artificial lighting to please the television cameras, for the deliberations are carried into every home by all electronic means. (The Electronic Parliament, e-parliament, and the electronics of democracy have given rise to a suite of new instruments 'e-petitioning', 'e-forum', 'e-democracy', 'e-government', supported by the public libraries of Scotland, for those without a computer at home, and the Parliament is the essential physical manifestation for the virtual.) That the assembly sits physically and metaphorically on the shoulders of the people in the vaulted public concourse beneath should always be on the minds of the MSPs.

In works of national significance the architect has a high sense of the delicate responsibility involved in structuring the frame for the play of the nation. Months of drawing and redrawing were necessary to find the ideal form for the Chamber. Any one of the plans could have sufficed but until the final resolution they lacked conceptual precision. The stage had to create the exact physical and emotional relationship between the MSPs as actors on stage, to shape the non oppositional consensual discourse that would enrich the making of laws in Scotland. Unlike music, which is only performed when desired and to an audience generally predisposed to the experience, the performance of architecture is in continual and ever present performance. For this Parliament the testing measure would not only be how people react to the space but also the ability of that space and that of the preceding movements, MSP Building and Garden Lobby, to stretch the imaginations and ambitions of the Members. The elaboration of the structure over the Chamber is much more symbol than support. The roof trusses have conventional member make-ups; compression-laminated oak beams and tension members in stainless steel.

> *The nodes are works of art in stainless steel welded plates and anchoring rods form meticulous pin joints. They have the scale and majestic power of the piston rods of great steam engines.*[45]

The expressive climax to this emotional performance is on the west side of the Chamber above the seat of the Presiding Officer, here the structure is carried across the assembly into a cascading glass roof and wall flooding the interior, the structure hanging suspended, floating in the light. The physical assembly of wood and steel rests not on any walls but is hung from an equally massive, triangulated, steel beam that surrounds the chamber. It is acceptable to read the symbolism of this and acknowledge that physical characteristics can be equated with an effective united political community. This compound array of different materials and elements conjoining to form a balanced and strong, yet stable order is a metaphor for the Parliament and the nation.

The end wall itself is a Miralles curve of arc and tangent containing the spatial drama in a diffuse skin of translucent timber. The galleries along the south edge, housing the press, dignitaries, and the public, sweep across the whole volume of the Chamber stepping down at one point to touch the floor of the House – blurring edges – 'sitting together'.[46]

It must be asked, if that was the intention, what response did Miralles predict? One would ask the same of any composer and the answer must always be – experience it and then you will understand. The more it is experienced the more it will reveal. The meaning is in the thing not what is said about it. The senses must not resist or disapprove if it is to be enjoyed. It is a conscious act to surround the Members with a feeling of exhilaration.

The most revealing view of the Parliament is from Salisbury Crags. Its embeddedness in the Old Town becomes clearer with every step up the Radical Road. The silhouettes of the National Monument and St Andrews House and the High School in their shadow hover uncertainly over the site; their detachment from the old city was never more graphic. For all its new and complex forms the new Parliament seems to evolve out of the history and the structure of the High Street and Queensberry House is allowed to be the clearest and the most sympathetic presence.

The place and its power is with the people. It is a quiet power, nothing demonstrative, as discussed elsewhere. The Palace of Holyrood seems to withdraw and be diminished by it. The politics in choosing to place the Parliament in the Canongate forced a direct confrontation with the Palace of Holyrood yet the new Parliament shows a quiet restraint to the buildings around it. (Imagine instead the Parliament as a free-standing monument rising up in the middle of this place creating unavoidable conflict with Holyrood.) As the new Parliament emerges out of the mass of stony Old Edinburgh, it pulls back to give great significance to Horse Wynd, drawing attention away from the forecourt of Holyrood. 'The chamber skewed off axis from the Palace repeats the Queensberry belvedere's haughty posturing.'[47] As the landscape develops, the effect will be theatrical and picturesque, an opening formed between the hard slopes of Arthur's Seat to the south and late medieval Canongate to the north, huddling beneath the steep face of Calton Hill and the dispassionate gaze of the High School.

On the east side of the Wynd, among the nondescript backs of the royal stables, a chapel has been converted into a little art gallery, carved over its entrance is a large, garishly gilded royal coat of arms – seeking the attention of the visitors to Parliament (by the laws of unintended consequences this overripe gesture makes the monarchy itself seem misplaced). The new landscape flows out of the floor of the Chamber, concrete shells carry swathes of grass into the Holyrood Park forming paths for walking and sitting together. Building and land dissolve into one. In Horse Wynd, Parliament and the Scottish Executive have created the first public park in the middle of Edinburgh since 1889.[48] It sits in the forecourt to Parliament and should become the stage for the nation's celebrations and protests – the forum of the nation.[49]

This wish to embed the new Parliament in the old city was limited by the request that the complex be enclosed with blast-proof walls and every part of the outer fabric bomb-hardened, making it more detached from the street than the architects would have wished (this was before the

September 11 2001 attack on New York City). However, in every other way the character and mood of the place retained a genuine affinity for the ancient city that surrounds it. Miralles observed, somewhat elliptically, that this would affirm 'that that the Parliament is already in other places'.[50] Each of the main spaces travels at different speeds, and that which moves most deliberately, measured and slow, is the public lobby – a dark passage into the future, moving away from Parliament and the Chamber into the landscape. The public enters Parliament from Horse Wynd. As conceived by Miralles, there would have been an uninterrupted flow of movement from the Wynd into the Main Hall but security demanded a narrowing path of entry through metal detectors. Once through, the public arrives in a quietly odd place formed beneath long concrete vaults. The geometry of the barrel vaults coincide and flow from the geometry of the tails of landscape – the land and the people enter the building together.[51] The surface of the vaults is embossed with a straggling, random series of distended St Andrews crosses and is carved into with soaring skylights in mysterious shapes. Here the stage is strange and unpredictable; it has a slightly religious air, a place to learn about Scotland and line up to enter the Chamber, a place for the singing of hymns, ancient and modern. (Its archaic character may resist its intended use as a setting for a continually changing display of photographs and digital media of the favourable state of the nation.)

Some may take the elevators, but the curious and energetic who chose to climb through the twisting passage of the public stairs will find themselves at the apex of the intersection of the Committee towers and the Chamber. Beneath layers of structure surrounding the stairs, the space is fragmented and kaleidoscopic. They then proceed by a quiet path to the Chamber and the public gallery, which almost surrounds the debating floor and shares equality in the spectacle of debate. The sunlight makes the

Chamber radiant and there is an aura to the space that gives worth even to the most modest issues. The mood is serious and filled with promise. (The ambition of the new Parliament was clear in the first wave of legislation: abolish university fees, give free personal care to the elderly, and begin a process of radical land reform giving communities the right to purchase the estates they live on.)

Approaching the Parliament down the High Street the buildings are completely at one with the character and texture of Old Edinburgh. Though an utterly foreign intrusion, its walls ambiguous beneath layers of shaped stone and concrete, it yet manages to be a natural presence, new yet somehow in spirit as old as the oldest structure on the street. This effect is enhanced by the restoration of Queensberry House onto the Canongate to its approximate shape in the seventeenth century, a complete recollection of the 'auld toon'. In its restored form it has been given a significance that it has not had in three hundred years, and did not have then for that matter. It provides a somewhat ambiguous connection to history, but a familiar symbol to which people can attach the idea of parliament. It is changed but not diminished by the new structures that surround it. It now forms the Members' working entrance. Before entering Horse Wynd the structures along the Canongate end dramatically with a sharply cut edge that opens to create a ritual entrance for the Scottish parliamentarians.

The Public Image: returning to Horse Wynd and the image of parliament in the popular imagination. The public entrance presents no familiar or picturesque view. It is an image formed from the canopy that flows out of the building to embrace and shelter the visitors beneath the sweeping curves of the main Chamber. The most distinctive element on the walls of the Chamber is the latticed wooden screen in front of the south windows, trimmed to the same ambiguous form as the stone panels that surround the walls of the complex save for the MSP Building. The form may be based on that of a curtain pulled back from a window, or the silhouette of a figure abstracted from life, these are conscious decorations that not only give movement and uncertainty to the surface of all the walls but also humanise its scale and presence.

Artifice comes easily to architects (in truth it is in the essence of the art, Baudelaire's reaction as the great terraces of Haussmann's Paris screened medieval squalor: 'Art veils mightily the terrors of the pit'). Miralles, as demonstrated in much of his work, had an ability to create sensational pictorial effects such as the giant gymnastic frame structures that enliven the streets of Barcelona – spectacular civic stage making – and the gravity and grace in the forms of the Igualada Cemetery. He could match effects to the meaning of the work making it appear witty and frivolous, ponderous and heroic as desired. Yet here he has consciously denied the Parliament of Scotland a familiar consumable image. When a lesser architect with a less wise client could have contrived a form, an image that could have popularised the project and the mission of government (playing with the stereotypes of Scottish history and character), Miralles has given a form to Parliament devoid of symbols (at least easily recognised symbols), devoid of answers of illusions, its forms representing nothing but its own nature. It is not a silent presence but whatever it is saying cannot be understood as yet, in this way it is reminiscent of Scharoun's Philharmonic Hall in Berlin.

I first visited Berlin in 1969 and though only three years since the Philharmonic opened it appeared naked and desolate on the raw edge of the divided city. As it has made its presence felt the Philharmonic has emerged as the most significant yet untamed work of architecture in the city in the twentieth century. Much of what I have written on the Scharoun seems to offer a way of understanding the Scottish Parliament.

As with the Philharmonic, the Parliament seems to be an object outside of history, a place speaking only of the circumstances of its own nature and use. Scharoun sought in the Philharmonic to make an object of renewal devoid of sentiment or nostalgia, or promises. In being hard to understand it would never be misunderstood. As with the Philharmonic, the architect of the Scottish Parliament has created an object promising nothing but itself. At this time and place in Scottish history and to a public wary of the easy promises of politicians, it is too early to say anything. As with the Philharmonic, what the Parliament will symbolise will be formed in the events of the history it makes; formed and reformed over the centuries in response to the laws made within it and its relation to the changing idea of Scotland. It is not shaped to be loved, to be immediately attractive, to make promises it cannot not keep, to toy with vulgar myths or to play with representations of history or culture, and it may never be comfortable. In the beginning was the word and the word gave meaning to order. The word described every element, every space and every surface in the syntax of ancient realms. Yet the Parliament belongs in the realm of a new reality which has moved outside the limits of the language. When there are no words to describe what is present, what will be the basis of understanding? This is, as it must be, an object for future time, to be as firm and as essential a presence as the High Street itself. It is intentionally new in every way and its aura and meaning for the nation will take years to form. It is a compelling and elaborate presence whose meaning it is left to the nation's collective imagination to decipher or create.

Consider that Donald Dewar recognising in this work the force of a new beginning, also knew that its presence would change attitudes and would not be immediately popular. It has reality which belongs and exists in and for Scotland; it has no equivalent. Its newness could reveal insecurity, conservatism and in some ways ignorance in the culture. An awkward yet brilliant work in its promise, the people must learn all its ways and nuances. In becoming familiar, one can envy those who in the future will help shape its meaning, see its character emerge. Relish the rare pleasure for everyone, politicians and public alike, of contributing to the formation of that meaning. The greatest works of architecture share with serious music a slow unravelling of significance. With every performance the layers of shifting texture and colour and mood slowly become acknowledged and felt. These buildings have a density that will take decades to be knowable and each generation will re-approach its meaning and significance in their own terms. Ambiguous maybe, but there are no deceptions in the self effacing presence of the new Parliament. It is unpredictable and thrilling in places but wholly for what it is, not for what it suggests or illustrates.

The Politics of Order: informal and circumstantial, connected only to itself and its place in the city. No ideal geometries, symmetries or orders from Westminster can regulate it. It is at ease with itself – it could not be anywhere else. Though perhaps not always understood or given respect, architects enjoy that dimension of their work that calls on them to be predictive, to literally build the future. Culture and society need such imagining even if it exaggerates or denies the emergence of other realities. To give form to a national parliament is among the noblest tasks that architecture can be called on to satisfy, and from the outset the Consultative Steering Group that formed the new Parliament was clear about one thing: this instrument of Scottish power must in no way resemble Westminster. They called for the design of a modern parliament which abandoned many of the traditions of the House of Commons: no proportional voting system, no more forcing coalitions, no one party commanding an absolute majority. It would be a parliament whose legislation drafted and debated in powerful committees, as in the US.

Unlike Westminster, the Members would sit in a hemicycle and not in opposing ranks, address each other by name (often by Christian name), vote by electronic buttons, and the first Scottish Parliament was 37% women (the highest in Europe save for Denmark and Sweden).[52] (This grew to 40% in 2003). MSPs would work daily hours allowing them to have a normal family life. This gave the conceptual frame through which to imagine a parliament for Scotland, one not in opposition to but distinctly different from Westminster.

Westminster in its monastic dress avoids the image of an autocratic centralised authority. The debating chamber laid out as a cathedral choir with its opposing ranges of benches matching exactly the oppositional nature of British Politics in the nineteenth century (Whig versus Tory): the Speaker refereeing from the middle, those outside the two main parties in opposition, the independents, having little or no influence. The structures of the Houses of Lords and Commons sit on the formative field of English political history, on the grounds of the Palace of Westminster begun by William the Conqueror in the eleventh century, and the Abbey of Westminster established shortly thereafter. Royal governance from the beginning tempered by the guidance of the church.

The British Parliament was itself the subject of a competition after the old parliament was destroyed by fire in 1834, (excitedly recorded by JM Turner). The parliamentary committee judging the entries rejected proposals in classical form – still much in vogue at the time – most reasonably because parliament would continue to sit within the medieval court of the Abbey. Classicism may also have been tainted by its popularity after the French Revolution. Instead they chose a vast medieval design brilliantly made but of a scale and form which would never have existed in history. From across the river, the ranges of tall perpendicular windows are broken by majestic towers creating a benign and approachable image for parliament. No bombast, no remote temples of power: an unexpectedly benign shape for the political centre of the world's most powerful nation. The design for the Capitol in Washington, only thirty years later, dominated by a domed pavilion (a confusion of the pantheon – place of all the gods – and St Peters) rising above a vast columned base, displays an ambition far in excess of the United States' place in the world in the mid-nineteenth century.

The plays of Westminster were and are bound to history and the past: the Miralles parliament would be shaped by the promise of the future; no historic illusions distort its reality. The deliberations within its halls and passages are as resilient as the fabric with which they are formed. The purposefully circuitous meandering of the circulation, from the individual MSP cells through the communal passages into the restless Garden Lobby, up the ritual staircase demanding an eloquence of movement and gesture and then down a quiet passage to enter obliquely into the Debating Chamber. The members seem to sidle in edgewise; nowhere the pomposity of strict symmetry and ordered grandeur.

Miralles consciously wanted the Parliament to be ahistorical, not simply in that it would make no reference to past or present styles of architecture, but in its desire to be wholly original. Its newness and persistent difference allowing it to exist always in the promise of the future (he somewhere uses the phrase 'the residue of the future' – not clear what this means, but its poetry is touching). This quality of being outside of history of realities is the antithesis of the decision in 1977 to have the new Parliament occupy the Royal High School. In advance of the referendum on devolution, the school was moved to a new location and the Property Services Agency prepared plans for its conversion.

The Royal High School was formed as a group of temples conceived as companion pieces to the project to build a replica of the Parthenon on the crest of Calton Hill, as a National Church which would dominate the city (the twelve glorious columns that the city managed to build do dominate and the ambiguity of their incompletion gives them a much more lively presence). The temples, galleries and terraces of the High School are not only grandly monumental and autocratic, they present a view of culture and politics that died with the nineteenth century (viva Scuola Regia). With respect to all that is powerful and new in the Miralles vision, the question must be why, merely a quarter of a century ago, a theatre of a dead past would have seemed a fitting setting for Scotland's future.[53]

The answer is there for all to see: The School sits in the shadow of a strange and silent monument intruding into the centre of Edinburgh – St Andrews House, the Scottish Office, from which Whitehall administered the affairs of the nation and housing the office until devolution, of its senior administrator, the Secretary of State for Scotland. (Before it was built Scotland was administered from a scattering of offices around Whitehall.) It was designed by Thomas Tait of Burnett Tait and Lorne in the mid-thirties and constructed between 1936 and 1939.[54] It was built in the aftermath of the depression which left Scotland with crippling unemployment, rising poverty and widespread distrust of the government in London. It was built to diffuse this discontent, to give the impression of a government closer to the people and their problems. It was built as war with Germany became unavoidable and Scots would be expected to serve and sacrifice. It is only with these conditions in mind that the ominous qualities of the building become clear (and the Miralles Parliament becomes a glorious antithesis). Its quiet and alien presence is insinuated so skillfully onto the landscape, yet it has always remained aloof and disinterested in where it was and whom it was serving. Donald Dewar wrote that even as Secretary of State he was always ill at ease within it.

Look closely: it was and remains a paradoxical and in some ways deceptive work. Its vast façade, though subdued, is wholly concerned with imperial symbolism, with representing the authority of Westminster and the Crown in Scotland. Its sole concern is with the imposition of authority from its lofty perch, barely touching the land, dominating but unengaged, making no attempt to be part of the city or the nation. There is more than a faint touch of colonialism here. See it as an imperial cruise ship (a Queen Mary in stone), the vessel of English authority docked against the slopes of Calton Hill, the bureaucrat passengers descending into the city now and again to watch the natives at play and buy their curios and strong drink. Or see it increasingly as having been an Emerald Palace, with the Secretary of State in the Thatcher years, just like the Wizard of Oz, sustaining this illusion of power and influence yet being able to do almost nothing for Scotland. It has only one obvious public entrance and that is oppressed beneath the monumental set piece of the façade beginning with the Royal Coat of Arms, out of which grows a parade of stone shafts crowned with figures representing what were presumed to be the virtues of Scottish culture: architecture, statecraft, health, agriculture and fisheries, and education (no philosophy, music or literature, and certainly not defence). And behind this vast declaration which speaks to an empty hillside, a small lobby; and filling all its terraces and towers, the offices of the civil servants. Despite appearances nowhere within this vast monumental edifice was there a gathering place for the people of Scotland.

It was the proximity of a usable debating chamber next to the Scottish Office and an acceptable image of authority that led to the Royal High School being named as the new setting for Parliament. This was in advance of the Referendum on Devolution in 1977. The referendum failed (political manipulation) but the High School remained the accepted symbol for the nation over the intervening years. Imagine the comments of some cynical English bureaucrat – 'Let them live with their absurd conceit 'The Athens of the North'.' In 1992 the Tories were unexpectedly returned to power in Westminster ending hope that a change of government would revive the promise of devolution and creating what was seen as a democratic deficit in Scotland: there were no Scottish Tory MPs. Following this a handful of disappointed men and women made their way to the gates of the School and after some days, set up a hut under a 'Democracy for Scotland' banner. They announced that they would stay there as long as it took for Scotland to be free, and so they did (significantly the police made no serious effort to interfere). 'The Vigil, which became one of the sites of Edinburgh, remained at the gates for over five years until the referendum of September 11 1997 released them from their oath'.[55]

The Royal High School, despite having commanded the southern aspect of the Hill for one hundred and eighty years, seems on reflection as detached from the reality of Edinburgh as St Andrews House. It has had a venerable and distinguished role in Scottish history that precedes its monumental occupation of the Calton Hill. It was certainly conceived as a project in the common good. It was both in image and fact a grand and ambitious institution, its classical garb worn with sincerity in the cause, cultivating ambition in the best of the city's youth.

What could be less appropriate for an ambitious, modern parliament than a nineteenth-century fantasy in praise of ancient democracy? Again the symbolic form of the High School was much more useful to those in power than an open vision for a new Scotland. It was political symbol, superficial, reflecting no deep interest or belief in a devolved parliament; it would have appeared like Stormont, a setting for a colonial administration. How more demanding yet necessary it was to create something totally new, both as an institution and as a structure. Such attempts at shaping the future in the fancy dress of the past could physically have disillusioned the cause. Had the High School become the new Parliament, it would have limited the ability to dream. Being forced to act on a stage built on a romantic illusion could not help but corrupt the dreams of the future. The extension of the Whitehall bureaucracy at the centre of the Scottish capital must have viewed the High School as a useful and token symbol for a Scottish Parliament in the shadow of the Scottish Office. There is, on looking back, a sense that the power would have remained with the bureaucracy. More troubling would have been the influence of the oppressive, cold monumentality of St Andrews House on both the vision dream of a free Scotland and on the day-to-day behaviour of the law makers.

The Miralles stage is a wilful divorce from an irrelevant yet significant past. A setting from which to observe the High School, St Andrews House and the slopes of the Calton Hill always aloof and above the fray. They were never to be part of the real city in the way the new Parliament already is. They never confronted the power structure implicit in the plan of Edinburgh, from Castle to park from military power to the political power of the monarch with St Giles holding sway, balance in the middle. The Miralles Parliament is the antithesis of Westminster, St Andrews House and the Royal High School; it may suggest how to think but not what to think. The Miralles-Dewar Parliament will force the nation to think for itself, to adjust to the shock of the new and believe in it, and both the building and the institution are able to be the direct reflection of the strength and achievements of those who use it.

In this fragment from the Hugh MacDiarmid poem, 'Why I became a Scottish Nationalist', he compares Scotland to a reluctant woman in bed. This could be an apt description of the popular reaction to the new building as each of us comes to know it and be:

> *. . . happy when after lang and sair*
> *Pursuit you yield yoursel' to me*
> *But wi' nae rapture, cauldly there,*
> *Open but glowern' callously,*
> *Yet slow but surely heat until*
> *You catch my flame against your will*
> *And the mureburn tak's the hill.*[56]

The architecture of this Parliament is brilliant and strong but not immediately appealing or desirous. It doesn't pander, doesn't divulge its secret easily, only in use will it surrender its charms, not by being looked at as an artefact but in performance.

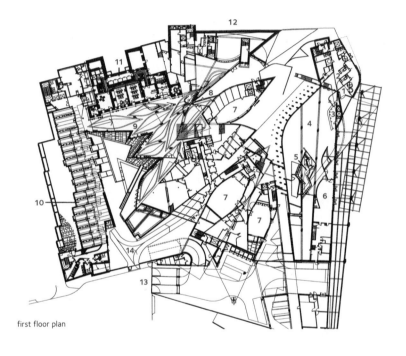

first floor plan

section at debating chamber

The Architecture

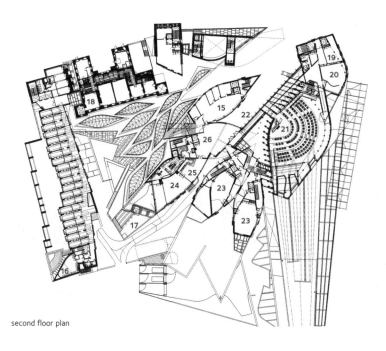

second floor plan

1	public entrance	**10**	members' office block	**19**	press room
2	security	**11**	Queensberry House	**20**	press conference room
3	reception	**12**	Canongate Wall	**21**	debating chamber
4	exhibitions	**13**	service entrance	**22**	bridge
5	shop	**14**	parking entrance	**23**	committee room
6	café	**15**	offices	**24**	dining room
7	tower	**16**	gym	**25**	bar
8	members' entrance	**17**	members' garden	**26**	lounge
9	members' concourse	**18**	Dewar Library		

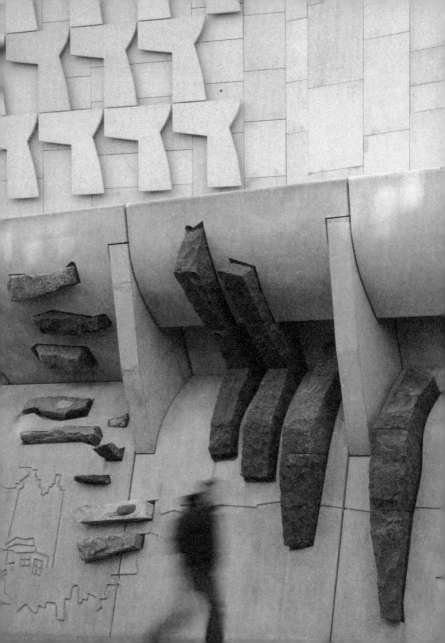

Parliaments Past

Looking over a thousand years of Scottish history there are only three significant settings of political power, all in Edinburgh all around the High Street – the Castle, in and about St Giles and the Palace of Holyrood at foot of the Canongate. (Though there was a fluttering romance among the city fathers in the nineteenth century with shaping the Calton Hill into a monumental political symbol, it never fully materialised.) There is an elegant completeness as the location of political power moves from the confines of the Castle into the shadow of St Giles and, after the Union, a century-long search for an appropriate national symbol which found a most unlikely resolution in the suite of buildings that bridges from Royal Scottish Academy to the High Street. (This remains a masterly piece of urban theatre, by one architect, William Playfair, over thirty years.) And what was created in the 1840s survived to become the home for the new Parliament in 1998. In the last act the new Parliament of Scotland frees itself from the monarchy and the church to return once again to the political and historic core of the nation on the High Street in the Canongate.

Edinburgh's medieval form was and remains one of the most explicit political structures of any European city – from the fortress on the hill to the royal hunting lodge at the edge of the deer park, it was from the earliest times formed and framed by royal power. Yet from the earliest days it was the church that dominated the centre of the city and had the most influence on the lives of the people. In its form and character the new Parliament is not only the antithesis of both Royal High and St Andrews House but also exists in opposition to all major structures that have arisen from political power in Scotland – the Castle, the Abbey, St Giles Church, the Palace, the Parliament Hall, the Tron Church, and Register House. The form and location of each of these structures was the result of a sequence of quite specific causes.

The Castle: the Castle Rock is presumed to have been fortified since the earliest days of human settlement but first comes to life in the chronicles of St Margaret, Queen of Scotland who died in 1093.[57] The twelfth-century chapel, that bears her name, is the earliest fragment of a complex of buildings which formed a royal palace over the next four hundred years.

It was while James II was still a child in 1434 that the first Great Chamber was built in the Castle. This formed the nucleus of the Palace apartments and was rebuilt and repositioned in the years 1496-1511 to achieve the form it retains to this day. The Chamber remains a grand tall space beneath a much restored and diminished hammer beam roof structure [58] (Illustration 1).

The only event of any political significance in the sixteenth-century life of the Castle was the decision by Mary Queen of Scots to give birth to her son James VI in the Royal Apartments in 1566. So beleaguered had she become that her reasons may well have been a need for security. One can imagine this beautiful woman (for many one of the grandest princesses of the Renaissance) never being able to adjust fully to Scotland after the extreme privilege and luxury of the French Court. Mary was forced to flee from Scotland in 1567 and never saw her son again. James escaped from the influence of his regents and assumed power in 1583; he made only a brief formal protest when Elizabeth executed his mother in 1587, by which act he became James VI of Scotland. As the son of the half sister of

Elizabeth, James Edward Stewart was acclaimed James I, King of England on the death of Elizabeth in 1603.

On his return to Scotland in 1617, James decided to hold court in the Castle and had the Great Chamber and the Royal Apartments renewed for the occasion, although he lodged in Holyrood. Thereafter the Castle played no further role in the politics of the nation moving over the centuries from fortress to national monument.[59]

The Abbey of Holyrood: the Augustinian Abbey of Holyrood had only a peripheral role in the political life of the country. It was founded in 1128 by David I of Scotland and rebuilt about 1220. In 1177 a papal legate travelled from Rome to hold Council there, so it must have had some national standing. King Robert the Bruce, Robert I, held parliament in the Abbey after his successful victory over the English in the battle of Bannockburn. The Bruce victory led in 1320 to the Declaration of Arbroath which was in the form of a letter from the powerful families of Scotland to the Pope pledging their support for the King. (Just to underline this action, the existence of Scotland had to be legitimised by the church in Rome.) This led in 1328 to the Treaty of Northampton and the recognition of Scotland's independence by the English.[60] The Abbey was the burial place of Scottish kings from the death of David II in 1370 to the interment of the murdered Henry Stewart, Lord Darnley, second husband of Queen Mary (and father of James VI) in 1566.

Its place in the nation was undermined by John Knox and the reformers and after the break with Rome brought an end to the celebration of the Mass. All the interior fittings connected to Catholic worship were removed from the abbey church with some anger and in 1570 the choir and transepts were torn down, leaving only the nave. Thereafter the Abbey was reduced to the role of the parish church of Canongate. It was briefly redressed for the Episcopal service that followed the Coronation of Charles I in 1633 (his English Coronation was in 1625). In 1687 it was to become central to the plans of James VII to devote Holyrood Abbey and the Palace to Roman Catholic study and worship, which resulted in the riots that gutted both in 1688. Its ruined state however is due not to religious conflict but negligence and incompetence – a stone roof installed in the renovations of 1766 collapsed ten years later and with the city focused on the creation of the New Town there was little interest in rebuilding.

The Palace of Holyrood House: the hunting lodge became a palace in 1377 and assumed its regal form in a series of building expansion between 1434 and 1511, the same years that the Royal Apartments in the Castle were also being extended (Illustration 2 – the site of the new Parliament is in the gardens on the left). It was built as a pleasure palace much influenced by the early Renaissance chateaux of northern France, both in performance and architecture. At its core it is mainly the work of James IV, dating from the start of the sixteenth century. He had married Margaret Tudor, daughter of the English King Henry VII, to strengthen relations with England and strove to make Holyrood an acceptable home for a wife who had grown up in the warm elegance of Hampton Court.[61]

His son James V died from despair over defeat in battle a week after the birth of his daughter Mary Queen of Scots in 1541; Mary was sent to France to be raised in the court of Henry III and his wife Catherine de Medici, not returning to Scotland until 1561.[62] In the intervening years, under the regency of her mother Mary of Guise, the Court moved from the Castle to the comfort of the Palace. During the years while his mother was captive of Queen Elizabeth, James VI expanded accommodation around an inner court with a mildly classical façade.

The Palace was the setting for the meetings of the Privy Council through the sixteenth and into the seventeenth century. James VI's son Charles I was crowned in the Palace in 1625, and after his execution in

1649, it was occupied for a decade by the Cromwellian troops of the Commonwealth. It played an intriguing political role, as will be seen, in the eighteenth century when, with the Act of Union, the monarchy essentially abandoned it.

St Giles stoically weathered the centuries of struggle between the churches of Scotland, England and Rome. Throughout the Middle Ages it was the only parish church within the burgh of Edinburgh. Its founding most probably coincides with the founding of the burgh around 1130, its scale and cruciform plan date to the years 1370-1420. The great church sits much more at the centre of the politics of the people than any of the royal structures (Illustration 3). From the 1360's, the representatives of the royal burghs established a continuing right to sit in Parliament with the powerful families and the churchmen, thus constituting the third of the 'Three Estates.' Throughout the Middle Ages the Parliament, unlike the English assembly, was essentially a roving feudal court with no structure attached to it, and Edinburgh one was of several cities seeking to become the royal capital. Perth was a leading contender until James II (1430-1460), who had been crowned in Holyrood, decided to hold his parliaments in the city (on the site adjacent to St Giles where the Tolbooth was erected in 1466). By the reign of his son James III (1460–88), a royal charter described Edinburgh as the 'principal burgh of our kingdom' and its established capital.

In the years of the young Queen Mary's absence in France, John Knox advanced the cause of Protestantism and in August 1560 the Scottish Parliament, in the cramped rooms adjoining St Giles Church, abolished papal authority and adopted 'The Confession of Faith Professed and Believed by the Protestants within the Realm of Scotland'. Mary, a passionate defender of the Church of Rome and still in the court of the French King, refused to ratify the legislation. The broadly representative General

Assembly of the Church emerged as the central legislative body and, in the First Book of Discipline (1560), John Knox and his ministers established a structure of ecclesiastical government for the Scottish people. This included broad social policies, including education and relief for poor, and was to mark the development of Scottish culture henceforth. Knox and the Queen had a lively debate on religion and the break with Rome, which was fully reported in Knox's *History of the Reformation of Religion*; Mary comes across as a spirited intelligence.[63]

Following the adoption of the Confession of Faith by the Scottish Parliament in 1560 all the medieval screens and furnishings were ripped out. The most immediate effect of the declaration was to find a way to accommodate 'the preaching of the Word.' Walls were built dividing the nave into four congregations each with the pulpit in the middle. These were taken down during the period that Charles I mandated that St Giles become the Cathedral Church of the Episcopalian See of Edinburgh (1633-1639). They were put back in 1639. Parliament had hovered in the shadow of St Giles since being established by James II: it shared the space in the old Tollbooth occupied by the Court of Sessions for its brief sittings, which was physically connected to the west end of the church. Following the events of 1560, in response to the threat by the Judiciary to move the Court to St Andrews, the Town Council moved court and parliament into the west end of St Giles itself. Charles I put an end to what he saw as a profanation and ordered the Town Council to build a Parliament House adjoining St Giles where the manses of the ministers had stood. (These it can be presumed had been vacated when the whole congregation of St Giles had walked out in protest over the actions of the King.)

The Parliament House: the Parliament of 1633 was an assemblage of the nobility and the clergy called together by the sovereign as the supreme legislative body in Scotland. Its only connection with the new

Parliament was that the Scots were managing their own affairs, but the power in the seventeenth century lay in the hands of a very few. In no sense was this representative parliament in today's terms; it was simply a stage to display royal protection of the law. The new construction was called on to house the Court of Session and the Privy Council of Scotland, with instruction 'to procure the same be abstracted forth in the Burgh to the grit lose and of the whole inhabitants of all degrees'. It was financed with a combination of public subscription and borrowing by the Town Council. Sir John Murray, Architect to the Court is recorded as having made the design, and though work began in 1632 it was not complete until 1639.

The Parliament as first constructed is well illustrated in several eighteenth-century engravings (Illustration 4). When one considers that it was Charles I who commissioned Inigo Jones to bring the Renaissance to England, and whose erudition helped shape the design of the Palace of Whitehall, which if completed would have been the grandest in Europe, this Scottish Parliament is a crude and provincial affair. The façade onto Parliament Square, despite the touches of uncertain classicism around the window towers and the main entrance, was crude and still largely late-medieval in character. Seeking no public attention or presence, its effect was insignificant and provincial. The interior in contrast, though still medieval was made impressive by the confidence of the multi-levelled hammer-beam structure supporting an almost flat roof. This was the work of John Scott, master-wright. Travelling from Whitehall and Hampton Court to make his obligatory visits to Edinburgh, Charles saw no need to bring his knowledge and pleasure in architecture with him.

On 28 February 1638 in the Greyfriars churchyard, in Edinburgh, a Covenant was inaugurated by leading Scottish churchmen. It reaffirmed Reformed faith and Presbyterian discipline and denounced the attempts by Charles I, with the support of the archbishop of Canterbury, to force the Scottish church to conform to English liturgical practice and church governance. In response the King chose to advance his ecclesiastical policy by force, but he was quickly outmanoeuvred and defeated by a well-organised Scottish Covenanting army. This first action would lead to civil war, the Crown against the Parliamentarians in England, the Crown against the Covenanters in Scotland. Charles was eventually captured and executed in front of the Banqueting Hall in Whitehall in 1649. It was in Parliament House in Edinburgh that his son Charles II was crowned King of Scotland in 1649 (this was twelve years before he would assume the English Crown, which is an aspect of the curious circumstance of having one monarch reigning separately in two nations).

The politics of this decision were a product of the continual search for clear royal endorsement of the rights of the Scottish Church as defined in the Covenant. The new King was willing to support the independence of the Scottish Church. The issue was and remains as political as it was religious. The church was the community leader, the minister, or pastor or priest was the agent. Under Roman Catholicism all priests owed their allegiance first to Rome. Within the Episcopalian Church all priests were in a sense in the service of the King. However, with the Presbyterian Church the ministers were appointed locally, though there were disputes as to whether the power lay within each congregation or with the local landlords. The Covenant would guarantee the Scottish Church the right to choose its ministers.[64]

The Tron Church: the Tron was just as much a product of the policies of Charles I as was Parliament House. Charles' decision, in 1637, to impose upon his northern kingdom a new liturgy based on the English Book of Common Prayer, although approved by the Scottish bishops, was met with widespread resistance within the congregations. When St Giles was made Cathedral Church of the Episcopalian See of Edinburgh, it was against the wishes of its influential Presbyterian congregation and they walked out or were ejected. They immediately began to plan the construction of a new church, the Tron. It was in construction from 1637 till 1640 under the direction of John Mylne, principle master mason to both the crown and the Town (Illustration 5). Facing boldly onto the High Street a few hundred yards east of St Giles, it is superior architecturally to the Parliament House. Its noble tower (a later addition) and classical facade made a grand public presence in the High Street. Dutch in influence with a veneer of classical modulations to its simple volume, it was a strong new presence. But its greatest power lay in the interior, aisles on three sides and a generous nave beneath a hammer-beam roof by the same John Scott, who structured the roof of Parliament House. But the roof slopes more steeply and the span is wider and the power of the space much greater. There is significance in the details, the roof of the Great Chamber in the Castle spans 33 feet, the hammer-beam roof of Parliament 49 feet and the similar structure in the Tron has a span of over 55 feet. Thus if political importance is reflected in the breadth of the stage for public assembly, the Tron dominates.[65]

The Tron was constructed by an independent congregation for their own church, a church based on Calvin's belief in equality of all souls before God: a church whose ecclesiastical power affected and mostly benefited the lives of the people much more directly than Parliament, whose self government was free from the autocratic control of the crown and the Church of England. Parliament was the privileged domain of the land owners, the law lords and Episcopal Bishops subject to the wishes of the king; the Tron was an assembly of the people under the leadership of their chosen ministers. Consider the Tron as the first major work of political architecture in Scotland. It was in a sermon in the Tron in 1693 that a Mr. Areskine was overheard praying 'Lord have mercy on fools and idiots and particularly on the magistrates of Edinburgh'.[66]

The Restoration of 1660 not only restored the monarchy but re-established the Scottish Parliament and Privy Council. With the restoration Charles II rescinded any agreement he may have made to protect the Scottish Church and proceeded to repeat the actions of his father. Between 1661 and 1689 St Giles was once again made the Cathedral of the Episcopalian administration for Edinburgh. The King took an active interest in remodelling and extending Parliament House and during his reign it became as much a place of public entertainment as for parliamentary and court business: a banquet was held there in the 1680s to honour his brother, James Stewart, the future James VII, on being named Commissioner of Scotland. The brief reign of James VII (James VII of Scots and James II of Great Britain and Ireland 1685–88), would bring Royal and religious politics onto the site of the new Parliament, into Queensberry House.

Queensberry House: in its earliest form Queensberry House was constructed by Dame Margaret Douglas of Balmakellie after the death of her husband in 1667. It contained both family and architectural connections to Northern Europe particularly Denmark. Dame Margaret sold the house in 1679 to Charles Maitland, Lord Hatton, who had to leave his 'grace and favour' accommodation in the Holyrood Palace when the future King James VII, an avid Catholic, was pressed to leave London for Edinburgh in the face of rising anti-Catholic feeling. The house sat almost at the gates of the palace. Maitland was brother and heir to John the Duke of Lauderdale, principal advisor to Charles II, in effect viceroy of Scotland, and deeply unpopular in both nations. In Scotland, he was ruthless in suppressing Covenanter resistance to the imposition of the episcopacy, though he himself had been a signatory to the Covenant in 1638.

(Parliament House is remembered at this time as a loathsome place to which the dissenters, mostly from the Lowlands, were brought before the Privy Council and tortured into confession.)

Charles II dissolved his last parliament in 1681. The following year the Duke died and Charles Maitland succeeded his brother to become the Third Earl of Lauderdale. He was appointed Lord Justice General of Scotland that same year and served until 1684. The King died in 1685 and was succeeded by his brother James VII. Charles Maitland sold the 'great mansion' to the First Duke in 1686. It can be adduced that his commitment to the service of the new King allowed him to stay within the Palace.

James VII quickly made his Roman Catholic sympathies known. In 1687, he dismissed his Anglican brothers-in-law the Earl of Clarendon and the Earl of Rochester. Magdalen College, Oxford was closed to all but Roman Catholics, a papal nuncio was officially accredited to St James's Palace, and the army was put under the command of Roman Catholic officers. In April James issued the so-called Declaration of Indulgence suspending all the laws against Roman Catholics and Protestant dissenters alike. In Scotland, the Council Chamber in Holyrood Palace was converted to a Roman Catholic Chapel and a Jesuit College was established in the Chancellors Lodge. In 1688, a mob gathered in the High Street angered at the aggressive intrusion of Roman Catholicism into the institutions of the church, the crowd rushed through the Canongate forcing its way into the Palace, and stripping it of all signs and symbols of Catholicism, (*the rags of popery* as the Scots would have it). As the rioters surged past the front door of Queensberry House, one wonders if some may have been tempted to take their anger out on a house so recently connected to the Maitlands and the King.[67] By then the Maitlands had fled and the new owner, the Duke of Queensberry was a noted Episcopalian.

The Convention of Estates: it was in Parliament House in 1689 that that the Convention of Estates declared that James VII and II had forfeited the throne and resolved to offer the Scottish Crown to the Dutch King William and Queen Mary. This gave Scotland a king who had no feelings for Scotland, save disdain. He curbed the political power of the Scottish Church by making its Ministry responsible to the Church of England. Queensberry was one of the early supporters of William III in Scotland; he held offices under him, rising to become commissioner to the Scottish Parliament (1700) and Secretary of State for Scotland (1702). William was succeeded in 1702 by Anne, sister of William's wife, Mary and daughter of James VII: another Stewart and a passionate Anglican (reigned until 1714). (Queensberry falsely accused John Murray, Duke of Atholl, of Jacobite activities for which he was dismissed by Anne in 1703, but she restored him to favour in 1705 with the offices of Lord Privy Seal and lord of the Treasury.) Queensbury worked hard for the Union with England as commissioner to the Scottish Parliament, and in 1708 he was created Duke of Dover (in the English peerage), and in 1709 was named Third Secretary of State for Great Britain. Thus, Queensberry House sat at the centre of political power in the years before the Union.

The removal of James VII did have one significant result: it permanently established Parliament as the ruling power of the land.

The Act of Union: war with France dominated the reign of William and Mary, and their successor, Anne, faced renewed conflict. Scotland's auld alliance with France was a continual concern to the English, making a union strategically and economically desirable. However, the neglect of Scotland by William and Mary and Anne led the Scottish Parliament to consider severingall connections with England. By 1707 England's pressing strategic concerns, and 'the nuisance value of the Scottish Parliament, were lively enough for England to offer statesmanlike concessions to

Scotland and material inducements to Scottish parliamentarians to accept union' – a union that would fully incorporate all Scottish affairs into Westminster.[68] The materials inducements were far from statesmanlike and in fact the noble parliamentarians were bribed – in a sense selling Scotland's independence to the English, though there were mitigating circumstances.[69] The Scots economy, weakened by a succession of bad harvests, and the failure of the Darien Scheme was in such bad shape that for the business leaders the Union was an economic necessity.[70] The Union did produce several clear benefits to the nation, it explicitly protected the independence and the administrative structure of the Church of Scotland and the independence of the Scottish legal system. 'Now there's an end to an auld sang' were the last words spoken in Parliament by the Chancellor of Scotland at the closing session on 24 April 1707.

With the Act of Union, the Scottish Parliament, which had met since 1639, was dissolved. Parliament House continued in use for social and occasionally political events until it was incorporated in to the activity of the expanded law courts. With the departure of Parliament and all the other apparatus of royal and representative public administration, Edinburgh was a capital without either the presence or the symbol of political power: a void at the centre of the idea of Scotland that would inspire a series of imaginative constructions all with the vision of the New Town.

The leading families of Scotland and England spent most of the year in London in the eighteenth century, and old Edinburgh, despite its romantic reputation, was a filthy and diseased place (it would be much worse a century later). Immediately after the Union, not only did the Parliament depart, but the monarchy appeared to lose all interest in Scotland and in the Palace of Holyrood House. There must have been a clear signal from London that maintaining a royal residence in the city was no longer necessary and soon after the departure the most powerful of the Scottish nobility moved in. The Dukes of Hamilton and Argyle took occupation as their right, as they had been named Keepers of the Palace, the Earls of Blackburn and others took possession claiming royal favour. The palace became an aristocratic apartment complex and one can only imagine its effect on the social life of the aristocracy. Consider that such a transformation might have helped shape the vision for a New Town. Here were Scotland's most powerful families living and entertaining in grand style, around a classical courtyard, a gracious hunting park on one side, a dense and decaying medieval city on the other. The noble landowners of London had been developing a more ordered city for decades – the squares and terraces around Lincoln's Inn and Queen Anne's Gate, would have been a continual reminder to the noble Scots of how much Edinburgh needed improving. The occupation of the Palace began in the first decades of the eighteenth century and was to continue well into the nineteenth, in other words throughout the time the New Town was conceived and developed.

There were only two occasions in all of the eighteenth century where the noble tenants were disturbed by royal affairs. In 1745 the Duke of Hamilton willingly rented out his apartment for the public reception of that most unlikely conqueror Charles Edward Stewart, 'Bonnie Prince Charlie', in his briefly successful conquest of Scotland. His success was a direct measure of the lack of interest in Scotland of the British court; the country had been left essentially undefended. However Scotland was not the prime objective of the invasion – this was a French supported attempt to overthrow the British state and restore the Stewart lineage.[71] Why this week indulgent puppet of France and the Roman Catholic Church should have become such a romantic figure in Scottish myth is inexplicable. (So peculiar was this last Jacobite rebellion that some historical perspective is necessary: it took place while Benjamin Franklin was corresponding with his English associates on the nature of electricity, the brothers Adam were still at the University of Edinburgh, and the idea of building a new town was forming in the imagination of Provost John Drummond.) The other disturbance to this noble apartment building was when a royal apartment in the Palace was made available to the brother of Louis XVI fleeing the French Revolution and his creditors.

In the years following the Union, the major physical structure that represented the politics of the people of Scotland was the Old Town of Edinburgh itself. The Old Town was at its most evolved as mapped in the middle of the eighteenth century (Illustration 7). The two major centres of power, the Castle and the Palace are just visible on the map, but hardly accessible. In a drawing by Paul Sandby from the same years, the castle terrace appears to have attracted a fashionable crowd. Some couples stroll, others gather and chat and show off their dogs and children; it is all very familiar despite the span of years that separates us, yet despite the sense of relaxation no one approaches the Castle's narrow bridge to the gatehouse, the only entrance (Illustration 8). By the eighteenth century the Castle is a restricted fortress, not in any sense a place of public assembly, and the Palace a private apartment block for powerful Scottish families (largely unconcerned with the plight of the many thousands condemned to a life of squalor in the stews of the Old Town).

The most overtly political aspect of the city's structure was the High Street itself, the broad public promenade at its most intense up from St Giles into the Lawnmarket (from the old Celtic word for open space), the ancient market of the city, enclosed by all the secular and religious wealth and power, coupled with the poverty and squalor that were intertwined in the heart of the nation. A structure of immense physical and all-embracing strength – decrepit it may have been but it was one

of the great main streets of Europe: a single unifying passage formed
between walls of buildings above continuous arcades, holding all layers
of society and industry. Its social and physical integration, despite the
squalor, forced a tolerant relationship between all layers of society; a single
unifying political and social structure, all held in balance and centred on
the High church of St Giles and Parliament Square. European visitors
wrote of admiringly of it: 'it was much more Northern French in
character than English'.[72]

The New Town: the congestion and squalor of the Old Town could
have been the most obvious reason for conceiving the New Town, but the
major stimulus came from the landlords concerned with expansion of the
city outside the burgh to the south. However, latent within this may have
been the need for the city to have a new identity, a new ambition to make
up for the loss of political power. The plan was formalised in the 'proposals
for carrying out certain public works in the city of Edinburgh', a statement
written by Sir Gilbert Elliot but shaped in the imagination of George
Drummond Lord Provost of the city, for the third time from 1750 – 1757.[73]
In 1767 the town council approved plans for the New Town as a residential
district (Illustration 6). The architect, James Craig, set out a grid five
streets deep and seven streets wide with a broad central axis terminating
in grand squares at each end. Princes Street, the southernmost of the
new streets, would be formed from a wall of residences looking south to
the castle. A. J. Youngson, in his splendid book *The Making of Classical
Edinburgh*, compares the Craig plan for Edinburgh with the plans for
Richelieu, Nancy, and of course with Bath and the piecemeal development
of the aristocratic properties in London.[74] Given the Scottish affinity with
France and distrust of England, Youngson assumed that the most obvious
influence would come from France. However, there were other new cities
and city expansions in Europe and America whose intentions and planning

effects were much closer to Craig's plan. Philadelphia, laid out in the 1680s (developed on land acquired by William Penn in 1681 coincidently in settling a debt incurred by Charles II), and Savannah, laid out in 1736 (General Oglethorpe), were both grid plans broken by garden squares and established against a rich set of political and social objectives. Drummond's prospectus for the new Edinburgh cites both, but more interesting is the reference to Berlin. The development of the western suburbs of Berlin were to have a strong influence on Edinburgh both in the nature of the task and in the final form of the results.

Berlin was the capital of a small ambitious state breaking out of the bonds of its medieval walls, first to give ordered grandeur to the palace and the gardens. Then from the 1680s into the middle of the eighteenth century, the west of the city was extended west in a grid of avenues and cross streets filling the land between the old town and the royal hunting park. These are built in a long terrace of noble houses with the main avenue to the palace becoming a new centre of civic and commercial activity. In scale and character Craig's plan is very similar; it lays out a simple, primarily residential order with George Street at the centre having the same generous civic presence as Unter den Linden.

The Old Town found its order over centuries of use and adjustment, a product of myriad transactions and compromises. By comparison, the New Town in its inception was shaped by one man and a committee, a simplistic 'ideal order' untested and unresponsive to anything other than a romance with reason (though admirable by some measures it is in many ways a cold and characterless arrangement). Where therefore is political power or public authority expressed in the Craig plan? The first explicitly political building in the New Town was Register House. The solemn and monumental Register House was the first construction in the New Town and served as both an anchor and a symbol of royal authority. Here were kept the public records of the nation – births, death, marriages – its contents defined the population of Scotland. It was designed by Robert Adam, Master of the King's works, in 1773. It was the first significant government building to be commissioned in the United Kingdom since William Kent's buildings for the Royal Horse Guards in 1750. (It was begun slightly before Somerset House, the register house of England, designed by William Chambers.) Before the Adam building, the public records of Scotland had been kept in the undercroft below the Court of Session beneath Parliament House and before that in the Castle (in this perhaps one sees modest steps towards democracy). Register House was the first free-standing, self-assertive government building in modern Scottish history. It formed a visual and physical cornerstone to the New Town standing square and central at the end of the bridge that would connect the old with the new. It was explicitly the presence of Royal Parliamentary power; its style was consciously neo classical, austere, fastidious and well mannered. As it evolved it not only held the public records but also told the time and indicated the direction of the wind.

This new suburb to Old Edinburgh was formed for the comfort and economic advantage of the elite. The intended presence of a church as focal point at either end of the major street, George Street, was more concerned with picturesque effect than with power of the church. That this is so is born out by the devious behaviour of one Lawrence Dundas who covertly gained possession of the most prized piece of land in the Craig Plan: the property that would end the easterly axis of George Street, set aside in Craig's mind to be the site for a great church. Dundas instead built himself a little palace designed by the most prestigious of the English classical architects, William Chambers. It is the only free standing pavilion in the New Town, a work that to this day seems to proclaim a public importance totally unrelated to its history. If one of the Georges had decided to have a presence in the New Town he could well have been satisfied with this. However, Dundas was a careless and flamboyant speculator, who briefly lost the house in a game of cards and had to give up other property to get it back. He died in 1787. To find the Dundas name attached to this palace at the centre of the plan one would not have been faulted for believing it to be Henry Lord Dundas, the singularly most powerful man in Scotland and its most corrupt; he was widely referred to as 'Harry the Ninth.' Yet his namesake was no relation, a completely different branch of the family. Perhaps he was acting in envy but his actions in creating such a devious monument, illustrate how little interest there was in the New Town or suburb as a political symbol. Imagine the New Town in the 1770s, the paths of Princes Street and George Street cleared and laid out. Only two new structures were to be seen, the shell of Register House, and behind it to the west the Dundas House.

The New Town entered the nineteenth century as an elegant yet hollow presence. It was slowly attracting the very wealthy and the new shops, and the musical evenings at the Assembly Halls in George Street were bringing the people down from the Old Town. Robert Burns wandered these new streets and the gaunt terraces of unoccupied buildings at the turn of the century and saw the grass growing in the middle of the street because so few carriages passed by. It was a place without any meaningful stage for the rituals and ceremonies of the nation. As the wealthy, in a trickle at first, then *en masse* moved to this rapidly expanding suburb, the impact on the society and the politics of the city was to create an extreme separation between rich and poor. Two realities: as the New Town developed and became grand, the Old Town declined into squalor, decay and disease, splitting the culture and the character of the people. The tenacious promotion of Princes Street attracting crowds on a Saturday morning, the wealthy, fussily dressed stepping down from their carriages, not knowing how to avoid the rabble that came across the bridges from the High Street and Grassmarket. The worst came up from the bothies clustered around the Shambles, the meat market in the valley below what became George IV Bridge. The new suburb now called town in a half hearted attempt to find a place for the lower classes developed 'colonies' (a name still used to this day) in out of the way patches of land where the more ambitious poor could be a small of this new world. By mid-century the New Town had drained all the wealth and energy out of auld Edinburgh, and apart from the ruinous conditions and overcrowding, it divided the classes so totally that even today the effects can be seen in the seams of poverty in the housing estates on the west of the city. (There is something of this schizophrenia in Stevenson's creation of Jekyll and Hyde).

The National Monument: there was a need to find a symbolic structure to give a sense of importance and focus to the New Town, a structure to give frisson, no matter how theatrical, to this hollow place. It emerged first in the dreams for Calton Hill (Illustration 9). It was the architect William Playfair who managed the evolution of the New Town to surround Calton Hill from 1818 onwards. In that year he designed a charming symmetrical temple to house the city observatory for the Astronomical Institution (recently founded by Playfair's uncle and guardian). Greek cross in plan with each wing strictly lined up to the cardinal points of the compass. He was then commissioned by the city to provide a plan for a new town between Edinburgh and Leith, which resulted in the extensive terraces that surround the hill north and south, Royal Terrace and Regent Terrace, developed and built in the 1820s. As these were being built, and well after the first terraces of the New Town were complete, grander visions for the city emerged that sought to give Edinburgh buildings of appropriate monumentality to confirm its place as the capital of a nation. These visions were driven principally by Lord Cockburn, Sir Walter Scott and, appropriately enough, Lord Elgin.

The British defeat of Napoleon, with its large loss of Scottish lives gave the excuse of creating on the summit of Calton Hill a national memorial.[75] In 1826 England's most revered classical architect C. R. Cockerel was asked to design the national monument. The words may have come from Scott, they gave precise instructions: the architect was called on 'to produce a facsimile of the Parthenon' to crown the Calton Hill, and fill the view east from Princes Street. (James Stewart first compared Edinburgh to Athens in his *Antiquities of Athens* published in 1772; a comparison at the time based solely on their similar topologies, many hills and a port not far off, but the Scottish Enlightenment enjoyed the conceit of reviving the instruments of an ancient democracy.)[76] It was conceived as a memorial for those who died in the Napoleonic wars, though it is described on maps variously over the years as the National Church and the National Monument. With Playfair supervising the construction, work began in 1826 but in 1829 the money ran out and the project was abandoned, leaving the residue of the dream in a flawless range of Doric columns in Craigleith Stone. Incomplete it is a much more poignant and picturesque mark on the Edinburgh skyline than had it been finished, but persistent embarrassment over the failure to complete, has oft times given it the nickname 'Edinburgh's Disgrace' and the idea of completing it has resurfaced occasionally over the years. It was clearly intended as a symbol of and for the nation, a structure representing the politics of a people who would wish to be governed by two forces, God and a romantic sense of Athenian democracy.

Sitting beneath the folly of the National Monument is the robustly perfect Royal High School, Thomas Hamilton's masterly composition. It is the grandest of classical fantasies, a product of the romance of the Scottish elite with ancient democracies – *build it and it will come*, carefully imitate the theatre of an ancient world and you will recover its virtues (as long as the ancient gods don't come with it).[77] But it was the ancient political, not theological virtues and values, that were being summoned up. In a romantic imagination such as Walter Scott's (a former pupil when the school was off the High Street, and part of the committee that created the new school) the High School would have been a symbol of *Pallas Edinensis,* the city *protectress*, goddess of war, handicraft, and practical reason, creating an urbane and civilised city culture. Yet when finally constructed in 1829 its elegant terraces would look over the worst slums of the city, as much a creation of the Enlightenment and the New Town. There is a poignant engraving from 1850 of a view of the High School from the Canongate. A woman is carrying her child across a yard surrounded by squalid houses, she must be walking close to where the Parliament now stands (Illustration 10). Whether intentional or not, the view of the temple complex emerging on the hill in the distance served only to exaggerate the squalor of the rotting medieval city, abandoned to poverty. A vision of the future, of the privileged few in their ordered new world, able to ignore those left behind. The new Parliament will emerge just to the west of the engraving of the nineteenth-century slums, restoring the political centre of the nation to the core of the old city.

All significant works of architecture are the product of the complex forces in culture. They are of most interest when created with a resolve to clarify such forces. The interest here is not just to show that certain kinds of political causes produce signal works of architecture, but also that understanding such causes and their formative effect on architecture reveals more about the artefacts of a culture than discussions of styles or artists. Just such forces are at work in the final set of public constructions.

The most extravagant piece of urban theatre in the city's political history can almost go unnoticed until pointed out and until one realises that it was, but one for serendipitous act, shaped by a single imagination. There are four parts:

1822-1831 The Royal Institution (now Royal Scottish Academy): through the 1820s Playfair emerged as the major imagination in giving form for the vision of a new town. The major symbolic structure was the classical temple on the garden side of Princes Street he conceived for the Board of Trustees for Manufactures and Fisheries, this to house the Royal Society of Edinburgh, the Institution for the Encouragement of the Fine Arts and the Scottish Society of Antiquaries, in 1822. Proposals to develop a range of buildings on the site had been put forward by Playfair and others in 1820 and a detailed proposal was prepared in 1822: 'a design that evinces in a high degree the classical taste and Scientific attainment that distinguished Playfair's labours'[78] (Illustrations 11 and 12). Playfair enlarged and strengthened the Royal Institution in 1831 while the city struggled over how to link the High Street with Princes Street up the mound of earth behind the Royal Institution.

1833 General Assembly of the Church of Scotland: the next element of the composition moves back to the High Street and to the politics of religion, the construction in 1833 of the hall of the General Assembly of the Church of Scotland the Tolbooth Church (it also housed the congregation of the Tolbooth). The architects were Gillespie Graham and a grateful A. W. N. Pugin (just after rescue from a shipwreck in the Forth). It was conceived as symbolising and confirming the unity of the Church of Scotland. It was positioned to dominate the skyline of the Old Town seen from Princes Street, its spire soaring above St Giles (Illustration 12). The site chosen allowed Graham and Pugin to place the spire exactly on the north-south axis of Playfair's recently expanded Royal

Institution. (This composition seems to knowingly carry forward the narrative explored on Calton Hill – the crucible of the national religion, the General Assembly of the Church of Scotland, rising in the distance above the temple of culture and industry in the Royal Scottish Institution.) Despite its forceful presence and determination to maintain a strong unified church, the year it opened in 1843, Church unity collapsed largely over the question of the congregation's right to approve its minister. The collapse became known as the Disruption, in which a third of the Church of Scotland clergy with their congregations left the Scottish Church to form the Free Church of Scotland.[79]

1845-1850 The New College and Assembly Hall: architecture is often the major benefactor in the laws of unintended consequences. Following the Disruption, the Free Church commissioned the building of their own College and Assembly Hall, and presented Playfair with the opportunity of conceiving a structure which would visibly diminish the power of the official church. He advised on the selection of a site on the crest of the Mound, highly visible from Princes Street and exactly in line between the Royal Institution and the Tolbooth Church. Although these were serious men, Playfair must have found pleasure and wit in using the spire of the old General Assembly Hall to give drama and distinction to the modest face of the New College. The Free Church claim of little means encouraged Playfair to place the force of the architecture in the theatrical silhouette of two towers rising above the massive strength of the Royal Institution, they frame and co-opt the powerful spire of the General Assembly Hall to complete the composition.

1848-1854 The National Gallery: Playfair's last major work in the New Town was the addition of a second temple to the Academy to house the Scottish National Gallery (again a commission from the Board of Trustees for Manufactures). These two grand vessels of Scottish Culture, now the Royal Scottish Academy and the National Gallery of Scotland, exude confidence and erudition. The resulting massive four part composition comes together, partly by chance, nudged by Playfair's imagination, to form a bridge between the old town and new, and create the illusion of the cultural nexus of the nation (Illustration 13). (Illusion only because there was never any cooperative relationship between the institutions with which he framed the composition.) The Scottish Church was reunited seventy years ago and the New College and Assembly Hall have maintained their imposing presence over the city.

The fates work in strange ways and, recognising that the New College and the Assembly Hall of the Free Church were in a sense the most genuinely Scottish political structures since the Union, there is something deeply satisfying in being chosen, albeit temporarily, to house the new Parliament of Scotland. Religion much more than party politics has defined the essential democratic polity of the nation. Since the mid-nineteenth century until the advent of the devolved parliament, the only significant political construction in the nation was St Andrews House. Perhaps it is too elliptical to speculate on the degree to which the continually active presence of these monumental figures, in harmonious opposition in and above Princes Street, has kept alive the desire for independence. It must be noted that for years the most vociferous arguments for home rule could be heard weekly beneath the colonnade of the Royal Academy, Edinburgh's Speakers Corner.

2004: A New Parliament for Scotland: this leap from the mid-nineteenth century into the present may seem far, but apart from the unconvincing presence of St. Andrews House, the governance of Scotland has had no structure, no tangible presence since the Act of Union – until the present.

And so two hundred years after the Union, the Parliament returns, not just to Edinburgh but to the core of the historic city, in a complex of buildings greater in strength and gravity than any that have gone before. They are the uncompromising structures of a new democracy whose all-embracing liberal vision has moved far beyond the distractions of classicism.

The Past

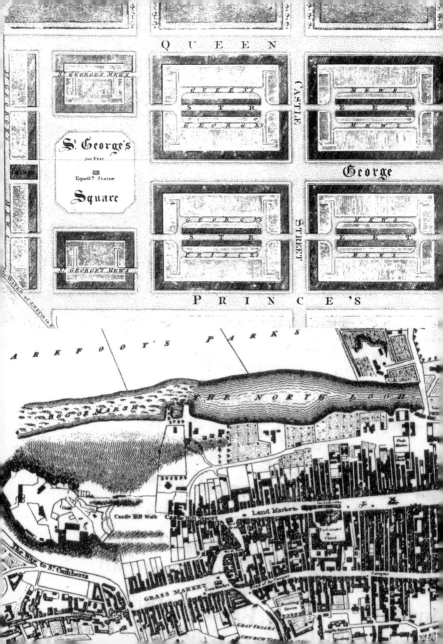

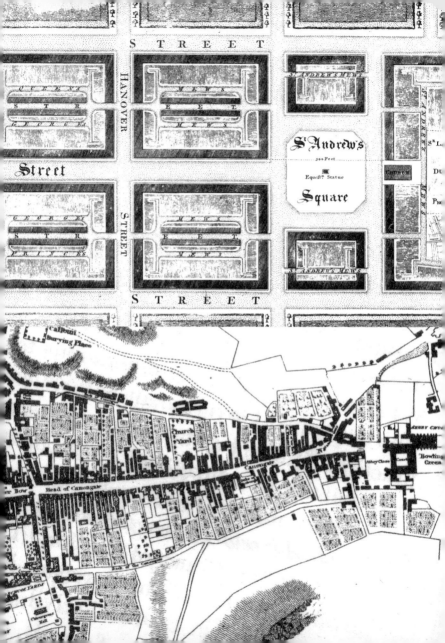

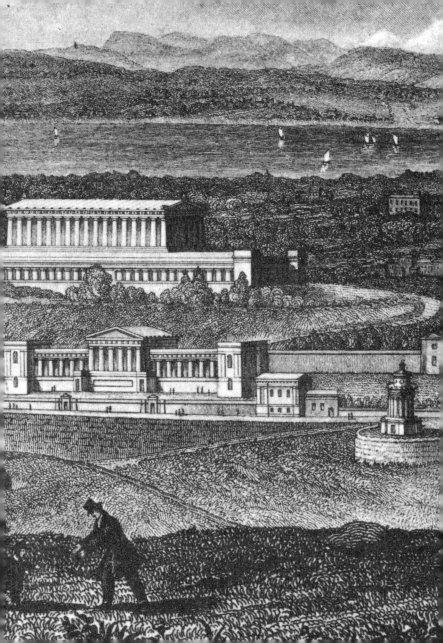

Epilogue: Parliament's Future

In the years after the Parliament opens, the silence of the buildings may take time to adjust to, particularly in the way they do not immediately accord with popular expectations. What was expected? Something familiar, reassuring, like something that had been seen before, something that accorded with the trivial myths of the nation (a hint of heather and tartan, and a scent of peat in the air). Any attempt to make the building a picture of government and politics would have by necessity have trivialised and caricatured the institution. Its nuanced ambiguity is hardly silence, more the subtle music of a choir in the distance whose words are just out of earshot, meaningful yet undecipherable. It will not always be this way. The meaning of the work lies in the hazy promise of the future. Century by century its significance will be continually revised and reinterpreted as it weathers the unpredictable and often violent storms of politics: imagine the parliament as the rock with the waves of political desire breaking continuously over it. Though physically it remains the same it is changed by association with the political plays of that it produces. Projecting the plays one hundred, five hundred years into the future helps to understand the Parliament in the present (buildings are time machines). Such projections are particularly easy in Edinburgh merely by looking at what has happened to St Giles in its seven-hundred-year existence. There is exact physical, textual and anecdotal evidence of how some things change and some remain the same; what is remembered and what is forgotten.

The residues of past futures: the core of the High Street has stood for over seven hundred years – and in the nineteenth century much of old Edinburgh was seen as slums built to last a thousand – so a work built to last one hundred years is able to stand five hundred years and more. A visitor to Edinburgh from 1640 when the first parliament was complete would recognise the place: cleaner and much less colourful – less intriguing, streets no longer crowded with people, horses, carriages, sedan chairs and the cries of street sellers – but the enclosing walls that made the High Street seem so secure remain much the same. And from one hundred and fifty years ago, the same walls, though crumbling and much diminished by disease and squalor in the flight of the wealthy to the New Town, these were the worst of times. Slow recovery through the twentieth century ended in legislation to protect and preserve the historic appearance of the street, as far in to the future as one dares to see. Thus unless buildings collapse through neglect (unlikely) or are destroyed by war or natural disaster – the volcano long dormant beneath Arthur's Seat suddenly erupts – this Old Town will increasingly resist change. From what is known now the Old Town and the New will, in all major ways, remain unchanged into the next century and beyond.

Fifty Years: the Canongate is now synonymous with Westminster. The whole area new and old occupied by the offices of the government and the offices of lobbyists and international agencies and even consular offices, gives the district a distinct sense of playing a part in the world game. The government's slow occupation of the surrounding areas was not without conflict. The most newsworthy came as work began to remove the tenants from the tenement block that adjoined the Parliament on the Canongate. Architecturally insignificant, early-twentieth-century-modest but the symbol of egalitarianism, of having poor families living right next to Parliament. In the end the families were left alone until they had all died or moved on. (For some such poor housing next to Parliament was unseemly, for others it was the belief in *a man's a man for a' tha*t). Following the example of Queensberry House the streets and buildings around are slowly returned, as precisely as possible, to Edinburgh in 1707. The careful and fond engravings from the eighteenth century become the building plans for the future, old stone facades rebuilt and forced to carry elaborate timber galleries, and the more complete the restoration the more powerful yet appropriate the Miralles construction seems.

The landscape bridge between the Parliament and the park is complete and at one with nature as the streams of shaped lawns seem to flow from the park into Parliament. A dense grove of trees echoes the semicircular terrace of the open air theatre, which has become a national shrine for the performance of the poetry and the music of Scotland. The east face of the Miralles building has darkened and if anything become more silent. The ritual significance of the place is emphasised by a screen of pennants and banners, but it is on the cobbled paving and the jagged pools of Horse Wynd that the nation remembers its heroes. The project began soon after the Parliament was finished and it called on works from the school of landscape sculpture peculiar to the Scotland that evolved for the imagination of Ian Hamilton Finlay. An evolving figural parade of Scottish worthies began to be assembled, in bronze and stone – portraits, striding figures, texts cleverly unfolding and some softly legible beneath the waters of the pools. They were joined by exquisite models, in miniature, in bronze, of the great houses by Adam and Mackintosh; by strange machines and primitive televisions and abstract files of viruses; and along with a sheep and the embryonic material that can clone us all. All very discreet among the swathes of grass and wildflowers in the patchwork of gardens and in the pools.

It is crowded on a summer's morning, people there just for the pleasantness and excitement of the place. It flashes in the sunlight with colour from the banners on the façade of Parliament to the sails of the children's boats in the pools, and seems continually in song and argument (singers of the music of Scotland no longer accept the term folk, it is world music in the tradition of Annie Lennox). And the setting has given rise to the production of epic poems written to be read loudly in Gaelic, Erse, and the much more accessible Lallans with all its pungent strength that English cannot rival (and with this the Scots have taken great pleasure in coining new unpronounceable words that they claim ancient sources for). At night under floodlights that slowly move across the curving masses of the Parliament changing colour ever so slowly to dramatise this place as the energetic, precious heart of the nation. And day and night the tradition for public debate, that for a hundred years entertained the crowds on the Princes Street in the shadow of the Royal Scottish Academy, was now bringing its sincere and sometimes eccentric arguments to the very door of Parliament.

The most impressive view of Parliament is from the top of the Radical Road on the north edge of the Salisbury Crags. Day and night it presents the most complete sense of how perfectly this construction sits with the city and the nation: Parliament in the foreground, the High Street rising to the Castle on the west and, beyond, the faint trace of the bridges over the Forth. Calton Hill rises dutifully behind the High School and St Andrews House, both looking subdued and servile to the pulsing masses of the debating Chamber and the adjoining towers. North in the far distance, the Parliament is seen against the hills of Fife, and east across the walls of the elegant apartments that line the coast at Leith the festive lights of the cruise liners in the estuary of the Forth.

A hundred years: the structures have weathered over the century making the images incised on the walls more poignant, and the darkness has increased the strangeness of the building, now much loved for obstinate fortitude that may be wishful thinking but which is seen as appropriate to Scottish character – this was never explicitly Miralles' intention. The Old and New Town is under the strictest preservation controls (every external stone and spar protected from change or alteration). They have become in essence museums. The High Street and the Canongate are closed to traffic, the cars held in large parking garages tucked into the hillsides north and south and serviced through a labyrinth of tunnels.

The land between the Parliament and the park to the south and west has become a setting for the creation of a most ambitious new town, this the result of a sequence of design competitions to mark the Centenary of devolution. The task was to form a vision and a master plan for the future (world respect for the Miralles' work made the Scots proud and willing to commission major creative figures internationally). The essential quality that was established with the decision to place the government between the land and the city gave rise to a broad commitment across Scottish culture to 'Design with Nature' (the proposition of that most prophetic Scottish ecologist Ian MacHarg). It began when the platform of the Trembling Earth was redeveloped to support a concentration of devices – wind turbines, solar collectors – all able to draw from the awkward Scottish weather enough power to make the Parliament self sufficient. The political symbolism was not lost as the nation continually evolved toward independence. This new Edinburgh evolves along the edge of the south-facing slopes of the park west of Parliament, in the extravagant commingling of natural and man-made order in which people live and work as if in an ideal but wild garden where the wind, rain and sun are made to give comfort and benefit. And through it all the Scottish

Parliament is a reassuring, if somewhat curmudgeonly, presence at the centre of the nation's place in the world: deeply respected and endlessly restored yet still recognisable though the dense forest that covers much of the park. It is a reassuring constant presence around which not much has changed.

Five hundred years: Parliament in the end is only diminished by becoming too small for the population. Imagine it sitting in the shadow of its successor a new building formed, to the disgust of those who would wish to separate religion from politics, in the most theatrical reconstruction of Herod's Temple spread across the crest of Salisbury Crags. Both the old Parliament and the Palace of Holyrood are joined in a tourist attraction; a cultural park and most visitors have only the vaguest sense of the difference in their respective ages or places in history.

Author's Note

I have four connections to the creation of a new Parliament for Scotland. I attended the Royal High School, for years the potential home for the Parliament. Painful memories of Saturday morning rugby practice on the playing fields of Canongate, now lying somewhere beneath the tails of landscape leading from the new Parliament into the Park. (In winter the ground was hard as iron, I have a sharp recollection of my classmate being carried off the field, his broken leg flopping sideways). Almost forty years ago I worked briefly with Robert Matthew Johnson Marshall and Partners. I have been a close friend and colleague of Mick Duncan since our college days. Mick, with his co-director Brian Stewart, has led the Scottish part of the design team that shaped the new buildings. I was also an acquaintance of Enric Miralles; he knew my writing on Berlin and for a few months in 1995 considered succeeding me as Chairman of the Architectural Association in London.

Apart from a short time in London, I have lived in America for the last forty years. Though I have returned to Edinburgh often, I had given little thought to the city until I was invited to write these essays. To nudge my memory I set out to walk from Princes Street to the Royal High School and then down by the New Calton Cemetery to the Parliament. There was an immediate rush of memories, the melancholy and strangeness of St Andrews House, the cold order of the High School. I was twelve years old when I first put on the black blazer with the arms of the city on its pocket and set out on my journey from Comely Bank to the Royal High, a journey repeated every week of every term for the next five years. The number 24 tram would stop at the foot of Frederick Street and I would walk briskly down Princes Street past Register House up Waterloo Place to the School. Five years in all weathers, gives plenty time to know and explore a place, to form lasting memories.

Over these years, I would often pause by the arch of the Regent Bridge, framing a theatrical and in a sense painful confrontation between the order of the New Town and the medieval past. Here framed in the elegant Palladian arch of the bridge I would look down on the black walls of tenements below, a reality that was no part of my world. Greenside, the worst slum in the city my mother claimed. Though I would pass close by every day, I would never have dreamed of going there. Further up I would pass the gates to the Old Calton Cemetery, cut in half by the construction of Waterloo Place, just a fragment on the north (its monuments moved to the New Calton Cemetery below the High School, just behind the Parliament). It was the profile of a standing Abraham Lincoln, glimpsed from the gate, freed slaves at his feet, that tempted me to linger there awhile after school. The tombs of the wealthy and powerful of eighteenth and nineteenth century Edinburgh were perfectly formed for the worship of ancestors, yet forgotten because in the all the years I can't remember seeing another soul, the tricks of memory can be revealing, they can also be wrong.

The bleak towers of the former house of the prison governor, forms a perfect bridge between the cemetery and St Andrews House, the Scottish Office, administering the public affairs of the country. Aloof, isolated: a coldness to match the prison on which it was built, I cannot recall seeing a single person entering or leaving the building, but then I always seem to be alone as I walked to the school. Compared with its neighbour, directly across the road from the entrance, St Andrews House was never mentioned in class. Though my art teacher took great pleasure in describing this little house, the studios of Hill and Adamson, as the cradle of photography – where they had made the portraits of every defector from the Church of Scotland following the Disruption of 1843 (that was his understanding).

As I look at it now the High School, despite having commanded the southern aspect of the Hill for a hundred and eighty years, seems to me as detached from the reality of Edinburgh as St Andrews House; I valued the education it gave me but it was a severe and competitive place and I have no fond memories (yet I regretted its move to an undistinguished new building on the outskirts of the city). I do recall several of the rituals and routines of High School life, the obligatory Latin, the smoking clubs in the tunnels beneath the assembly hall, the procession of graduates through the great doors of the hall, which were opened but once a year just for them. During the second, or at the beginning of third year, I recall that every class had to run round the Calton Hill once a week, come rain or snow or shine. I never seemed to be warmly enough dressed as I stumbled up the steps just up from the Hill Adamson House, past the tomb of Dugald Stewart and the little temple housing the Royal Scottish Observatory, on past the enormous and gracious columns of Edinburgh's Parthenon (always seeming to me to be larger than the real thing). Passing by the gardens laid out by Patrick Geddes for the communal pleasure of those privileged tenants of Regent Terrace, and then back along the path above the school. This is a remarkable place yet I don't think there was much attempt by teachers in literature or history or art to explain why we were part of such an extravagant classical theatre.

The last part of my walk begins by the railings at the Burns Memorial then down into the New Calton Cemetery; this is still a lost place with such an air of sadness. We would take a variety of paths down to the playing field, and buy little packs of the cheapest cigarettes in the Canongate and smoke them in the hidden corners of Whitehorse Close.

What is so extraordinary today is not how little has changed but how clearly appropriate to this place, despite their difference, are the buildings of this strong new Parliament.

Devolving Scotland

1   The reference is to the Book of Judges (12,6), where the Gileadites identified and slew the Ephraimites on the basis of their inability to pronounce the word: 'Then said they unto him, Say now Shibboleth; and he said Sibboleth; for he could not frame to pronounce it right. Then he took him, and slew him at the passages of the Jordan: and there fell at that time of the Ephraimites forty and two thousand.' (King James Version).

2   Miles Glendinning et al., *A History of Scottish Architecture*, Edinburgh University Press, 1996, p.202.

3   Jonathan Hearn, 'Big City: civic symbolism and Scottish Nationalism', in *Scottish Affairs*, 42, 2003, p.65.

4   Benedict Anderson's phrase, the title of his book *Imagined Communities: reflections on the origin and spread of nationalism*, Verso, London, 1996.

5   Scottish Social Attitudes surveys are reported in a series of books including: L. Paterson et al., *New Scotland, New Politics?* Polygon, Edinburgh, 2001; J. Curtice et al., *New Scotland, New Society?* Polygon, Edinburgh, 2002; C. Bromley et al., *Devolution – Scottish Answers to Scottish Questions?* Edinburgh University Press, 2003.

6   Since 1999, around 6 out of 10 people have consistently agreed that the Scottish Parliament should be given more powers.

7   NFO System Three for *The Herald* reported on 7 July 2003.

8   B. Tagliabue, (ed.) *Enric Miralles, Works and Projects, 1975-1995,* New York: The Monacelli Press, 1996, p7; quoted in C. Hermansen, 'The New Scottish Parliament Building by Miralles-Tagliabue Architects', Mac Journal Five.

9   P. Robertson, *Charles Rennie Mackintosh: art is the flower,* Pavilion Books, London, 2002.

10   Kathleen Jamie, 'For a new Scottish Parliament', in *Without Day: proposals for a new Scottish Parliament*, pocketbooks, Edinburgh, 2000.

11   The German social theorist Max Weber made the distinction between 'force' and 'authority', macht and herrschaft, the basis of his analysis of social power at the beginning of the 20th century, in his magnum opus, *Economy and Society*.

12   C. R. Wickham-Jones, *Arthur's Seat and Holyrood Park: a visitor's guide*, HMSO, 1996, ch.4.

13   Ibid.

14   Holyrood Inquiry, transcript, 26 Nov 2003, para.120.

15   Queensberry House now holds the Donald Dewar book collection which was bequeathed to the Parliament by the Dewar family.

16   Neal Ascherson has made this the central theme of his book *Stone Voices*, which treats Scotland itself as archaeological metaphor, stratified layers of meanings and identities passed down through ages and shaped into new forms by later generations, but never quite losing the residues of the old.

17   J. Hunter, *The Making of the Crofting Community*, John Donald, Edinburgh, 1976.

18   Sir David Steel, the first Presiding Officer of the Scottish Parliament, addressed the monarch as 'Queen of Scots' at the formal opening of the Parliament on 1 July 1999.

Deliverance Comes

19   Neal Ascherson *The Stone Voices: The Search for Scotland,* p30, Hill and Wang a division of Farra, Straus Giroux New York 2002.

20   EMBT RMJM documents.

21   Enric Miralles in conversation with Emilio Tunon & Luis Moreno Mansilla *Notes on an Informal Conversation* (The last interview before his death in June of 2000) In *Croquis* 2000, n.100-101.

22   The problem with the musical analogy is that it works perfectly with Beethoven but with very few contemporary composers. John Adams in the US, Boulez in France, yet perhaps there are as few major architects as there are composers. Miralles was 44 when he died there are no major composers as young.

23   This was particularly evident in the trivial quality of so many of the submissions for the memorial on the site the World Trade Centre. There are exceptions, James Tyrell being the most obvious in the US and that of Ian Hamilton Finlay.

24   The last decade of the 20th century saw major works in Berlin, London, Los Angeles, and Bilbao garner enormous world interest. These then are the best of times for the unveiling of a significant work of political architecture.

25   *A conversation with Enric Miralles* with Alejanadro Zaera. In *Croquis* 1995, n.72 (pt.2).

26   Ibid.

27   Donald Dewar's jury was: Dr John E Gibbons, Director of Building Scottish Office; Joan O'Connor Architect, Past President RIAI; Robert Gordon, Head of Constitution Group Scottish Office; Kirsty Wark, Journalist & Broadcaster; Professor Andy McMillan, Head of Macintosh School of Architecture.

28   He had studied English in Edinburgh as a young man and was a popular visiting critic at the Mackintosh school in Glasgow years before the competition. He had a deep fondness for the work of the Scottish architect Charles Rennie Mackintosh, seeing parallels in it to the Catalan architect Antonio Gaudi; The Glasgow College of Art, now the Mackintosh School, is still Mackintosh's greatest work.

29   The 35 people who lived on Hirta, the largest of the islands, were evacuated in 1930, thus ending settlement on the island that had been continuous since prehistoric times.

30   They had been traced from a photograph he had taken at Lindisfarne in Northumberland, a place from which Southern Scotland was Christianised.

31   From notes made by Mick Duncan, the editor of this work and Miralles' close colleague in the Scottish side of the partnership.

32   There are two difficulties in transcribing Miralles' notes, first his handwriting is small and he sometimes leaves out a letter and, secondly, he does not aim for exact English, for example in the previous quote he wrote 'parliament sit in the land.' For legibility where the correct form is obvious it has been used.

33   This celebration of the finished work and the quality and character of this book are due to the imagination and dedication of Mick Duncan, and is tangible representation of his admiration for Enric Miralles.

34   Mick Duncan, op cit.

35   Mick Duncan, op cit.

36   Historic Scotland safeguards the nation's built heritage and promotes its understanding and enjoyment on behalf of Scottish Ministers.

37   Ascherson, p.292 op cit. from the *Collected Poems* by Louis MacNeice, Faber and Faber.

Wisdom, Justice, Compassion, Integrity

38   Apart form the College of Art, Mackintosh was never commissioned to create a work of national importance in Scotland.

39   There are many gifted architects in Scotland, particularly among the new generation, and commissions are becoming much more interesting and ambitious.

40   Antoni Gaudi (Catalan), born June 25, 1852, Reus, Spain, died June 10, 1926, Barcelona. His work has parallels with *Arts Nouveau Movement* in Northern Europe but in Spain is called *Moderisme* having freedom of form, voluptuous colour and texture, and organic unity. His productive career was dominated with the construction of the Expiatory Temple of the Holy Family (Sagrada Familia), which was unfinished at his death in 1926.

41   Comparisons can be made to the work of Steven Holl or the middle period of Frank Gehry's work; he shares with Peter Eisenmann the distinction of having a Doctoral degree in architecture.

42   David Mackay on Gaudi *Contemporary Architects,* St Martins Press.

43   These are drawn from notes made by Mick Duncan, Miralles' closest colleague in the Scottish side of the partnership.

44   Ibid.

45   Ibid.

46   Ibid.

47   Mick Duncan, op. cit.

48   Inverleith.

49   Mick Duncan, op. cit.

50   Ibid.

51   Ibid.

52   See Neal Ascherson, op. cit. p.293. Westminster retains Foreign and Defence policy, Constitution, Immigration, Trade, Macro Economics and Broadcasting. Scotland has the rest: Housing, Education, Farming, Health and Social Services, Fisheries, Culture, Sport, Law. These programmes are supported by a block grant from London supplemented if the Scottish Parliament so desires by a surcharge on Income Tax.

53   There is an apt quote from Abraham Lincoln: 'One must abandon the quiet dogma of the past to face the stormy realities of the present'.

54   St Andrews House arrives out of nowhere and nothing in Scotland. Its forms are
      conservative *Moderne* faint echoes of F. L. Wright and even Dudok.

55   Neal Ascherson, *Stone Voices,* op. cit.

56   From Hugh MacDiarmid's *Complete Works,* Carcanet Press.

Parliaments Past

57   Wife of Malcolm Canmore who defeated and killed Macbeth.

58   Stirling Castle had a similar hall.

59   Military conflict with England throughout the 16th and with France in the 17th
      and 18th century demanded that the castle become principally an instrument of
      war, and this produced ever widening of the layers of curtain defences. It is possible
      to forget that the romantic pile at the centre of the life of the city saw centuries of
      warfare. By the 18th century the royal chamber had been converted into an arsenal
      with an adjoining canon foundry. By the 19th century threats of war had passed and
      the castle gradually assumed the role it plays to day offering a romantic experience
      with the conflicts that have marked Scottish history.

60   The following year the Pope granted to the independent kings of Scots the right
      to be anointed with holy oil, but that year also Robert died.

61   He was also aware of the elegance of foreign courts, where he was respected.
      He patronised literature, licensed Scotland's first printers, and improved education.

62   Half sister of Elizabeth, both daughters of Henry VIII. Mary was raised in a deeply
      Catholic court; Elizabeth defended the English Church created by her father.
      A suspicion that the Catholic action would seek to have Mary take the throne from
      Elizabeth persisted and Mary, despite her appeals to France, became the prisoner
      of Elizabeth and was forced to surrender the Scottish crown in 1585 and was then
      executed, her son being named King James VI on her death.

63   www.reformed.org/documents/knox/knox to mary.html

64   An original copy of the Covenant lies unheralded framed behind glass in a corner
      of St Giles. When I enquired in the bookstore and of a church official if there was an
      explanation or a printed version, I was told that there nothing in St Giles but I could
      try Greyfriars.

65 Though it must be added that the Tron was shorter in length than the Parliament, 52 feet as opposed to 82 and now shorted by two bays; it is hard to compare it with Parliament or imagine the forceful presence it once was. The current condition (2004) of the Tron is a travesty, its walls stripped, its floor dug up to show the foundations of the medieval lane that had once passed though this space. Yet most troubling of all are the information boards put up by the city which claim that the Tron was built on the orders of Charles I to take the overspill population from St Giles. This essay depends on secondary material but nothing in the scholarly record supports this. Are the authorities still unwilling to criticise the monarchy?

66 Charles McKean, *Edinburgh, An Illustrated Architectural Guide* 24, RIAS 1992, Edinburgh.

67 Charles Maitland fought with James at the Battle of the Boyne and after the defeat fled to exile in France where he died in 1691.

68 John Simpson, *Scotland Encyclopaedia Britannica*.

69 The Scottish Parliament was ended and the Westminster Parliament increased by 45 commoners and 16 peers representing Scotland. Scotland benefited by gaining free trade with England and its colonies, by the grant of a money 'Equivalent' of the share of the English national debt that Scotland would assume.

70 The Darien Scheme was the Scottish financed establishment of a productive colony in Panama.

71 The threat had been serious at first when the French launched a fleet in support of the Stewart cause to invade Scotland, but it was battered severely in a storm and never made land.

72 Also at the centre of the map the Tron Church as discussed earlier the first modern political work of architecture in the city really. The map was prepared before the second modern building was complete, the Royal Exchange. It was completed in 1753 immediately opposite St Giles, to the designs of John Adam father of Robert. Its façade was the first mark of a confident new classicism that would compel the imagination and define a new reality for Scotland well into the next century). Though it had the appearance of a public structure it was in fact a speculative venture that failed, the merchants of the city preferring to do business on the High Street. Its failure could also have been due to a feeling of resentment at the presence of such an alien structure in the High Street. This was the first and last attempt to insert major work in the new style within the old town.

73 He strongly opposed the Jacobite invasion and joined Copes Army: the English army, in putting an end to it.

Hey Jonnie cope are ye wauking yet
Or are your drums a – beating yet?
If you were wauking I would wait,
Tae gang tae The Coals in the morning

74 A.J. Youngson's *The Making of Classical Edinburgh.* This is the most substantial document of Edinburgh's history and one of the most satisfying works of urban scholarship.

75 First a rather ungainly circular tower was built in 1807 (William Burns) to commemorate the Battle of Trafalgar.

76 James Stewart, and Nicolas Revett *The Antiquities of Athens* in a series of editions published in 1762, 1789, 1795. For all the formality with which the Scottish viewed the bible and Christianity, the extravagant pleasure of creating houses of worship in classical dress suggests either a promiscuous view of reality or strong streak of Platonism.

77 In the case of the High School the language of the architecture was matched by having the pupils speak Latin and the brightest expected to speak Greek.

78 Youngson, op. cit.

79 When parliament restored patronage to Scotland in 1712 congregations lost the right to choose their preacher, which was given instead to the landowners. This 66 act brought the Church under the influence of the moderates. Dissention between moderates and evangelicals festered for over a century or more and the bitterness of the disputes after 1833 led to the Disruption of 1843; the dissenters leaving the official Church to form the Free Church of Scotland. Patronage was abolished in the choice of a minister in 1884 and with further changes in national policy in 1921 left the Church of Scotland as the national but not the State church. In 1929 the two churches reunited as the Church of Scotland.

Illustrations

Chapter 1: Enric Miralles' drawings are reproduced with the kind permission of Benedetta Tagliabue and the Scottish Parliament Corporate Body.

Chapter 2: All photography copyright of Duccio Malagamba-fotografia de arquitectura S.L.

Sources of the historical material in chapter 3 are as follows:

1   The Interior Quadrangle of the Castle, Edinburgh; showing the door leading to the apartment where Queen Mary was confined also the room where the regalia was discovered. Drawn by Tho. H Shepherd and engraved by J. Hinchliff. Collection of the author.

2   This is described in *Old & New Edinburgh* as being 'Holyrood Palace and Abbey from the rare View by Hollar in the British Museum' from the collection of Peter Stubbs, (EdinPhoto) with permission. (I cannot verify this but Wenzel Hollar was one of the most celebrated engravers of the 17th century, known in London particularly for his illustrations of London after the great fire. He was born 1607 in Prague and died in London in 1677.)

3   St. Giles Kirk and The High Street Edinburgh from a drawing by J. M. W. Turner, engraved by H. Le Keux, the figures engraved by G. Cooke. Published 19 December 1819, London. Collection of the author.

4   Parliament Square, John Elphinstones' view of c.1750, prepared for Hugo Arnot's *History of Edinburgh* published 1779, from A. J. Youngson *The Making of Classical Edinburgh*, Edinburgh University Press.

5   A Perspective View of the Front of the Tron Kirk with the Adjoining Buildings, John Elphinstone Esq. Engineer delin. Collection of the author.

6   James Craig 'Plan of the new streets and squares intended for the City of Edinburgh 1767', from A. J. Youngson, *The Making of Classical Edinburgh*, Edinburgh University Press. Collection of the author.

7   Map of Edinburgh in mid-18th century, from A. J. Youngson, *The Making of Classical Edinburgh*, Edinburgh University Press.

8   Edinburgh Castle in the mid-18th century, Paul Sandby, collection of the author.

9   Playfair's vision for Calton Hill complex completed, from A. J. Youngson, *The Making of Classical Edinburgh*, Edinburgh University Press.

10   The Royal High School from the Canongate, c.1840s, from the collection of Peter Stubbs, (EdinPhoto) with permission.

11   The Royal Scottish Academy and the National Gallery of Scotland drawn by their architect Playfair, from A. J. Youngson, *The Making of Classical Edinburgh*, Edinburgh University Press.

12   Princes Street looking west, before the building of the Royal Institution, by Kay, from A. J. Youngson, *The Making of Classical Edinburgh*, Edinburgh University Press.

13   View of the Mound from Hanover Street showing the Royal Academy and, behind that, the New College and Assembly Hall, and in the distance the spire of the Tolbooth Church. From a 19th century postcard by G.W. Wilson, from the collection of Peter Stubbs, (EdinPhoto) with permission.

Acknowledgements and Permissions

The extract from Neal Ascherson *The Stone voices: The Search for Scotland*, published by GRANTA, (London 2002). It appears with the kind permission of the publishers. *Stone Voices* could not have arrived at a more opportune time for me as it provided the most emotional reintroduction to the awkwardness and strengths of the Scottish character. I am also in Ascherson's debt for the extracts from two extraordinary poems.

Permission is pending for the Louis MacNeice poem 'The Autumn Journal' from *Collected Poems, 1925-1948*, published by Faber and Faber, London 1949. Hugh MacDiarmid's 'Why I became a Scottish Nationalist' from his *Complete Poems*, appears by permission of Carcarnet Press.

The extensive quotes from the Miralles drawings are reproduced with the kind permission of Benedetta Tagliabue and The Scottish Parliament Corporate Body. The text of his final letter to the team is published with the permission of Michael Duncan.

The format of this book is a homage to the successful *pocketbooks* series on Scottish Culture conceived by Alec Finlay and designed by Lucy Richards of StudioLR.

Biographies

George Reid is the Presiding Officer of the Scottish Parliament. He has no party allegiance while in his post. Educated at Dollar Academy, he has an MA(Hons) 1st Class in History, from St Andrew's University in 1962, and a Diploma in International Relations Union College in the USA.

After university he worked as a journalist and producer for the BBC, Granada Television, STV and a number of newspapers. For 12 years he was Director of Public Affairs for the International Red Cross and Red Crescent, based in Geneva but working worldwide in conflict and disaster zones.

He was MP for Clackmannan and East Stirlingshire from 1974–79, and simultaneously Member of the Assembly of the Council of Europe. Appointed to the Steering Group for the Scottish Parliament, to which in 1999 he was elected as regional MSP for Mid Scotland and Fife and subsequently as Deputy Presiding Officer. In 2003 he was elected constituency MSP for Ochil and subsequently as Presiding Officer.

David McCrone is Professor of Sociology, and director of the University of Edinburgh's Institute of Governance. He is a Fellow of the Royal Society of Edinburgh. He is coordinator of the research programme funded by The Leverhulme Trust on Constitutional Change and National Identity (1999-2004), and was vice-chair of ESRC's Research Priorities Board (2000-2004). He was a member of the Expert Panel which devised procedures and standing orders for the Scottish Parliament, and was advisor to its Procedures Committee which reviewed the parliament's founding principles.

He has written extensively on the sociology and politics of Scotland, and the comparative study of nationalism. His recent books include: *Living in Scotland: social and economic change since 1980* (2004); *Understanding Scotland: the sociology of a nation* (2001); *New Scotland, New Society?* (2001), *New Scotland: New Politics?* (2000); and *The Sociology of Nationalism: tomorrow's ancestors* (1998).

Alan Balfour is an architect and author. He was born in Edinburgh and attended the Royal High School and Edinburgh College of Art (he won the Edinburgh Corporation Medal for Civic Design in 1961). He attended Princeton University as a Fulbright Scholar.

His most recent books are *Shanghai* in 2002 and *New York* in 2001, both in the World Cities series published by Wiley/Academy, London. They offer critical histories of city character and form as defined by the architecture. The first in the series, *Berlin* published by Academy Editions in 1995, documents the transformation of Berlin before and after the collapse of the 'Wall'. This and the earlier book *Berlin: The Politics of Order: 1737–1989* (Rizzoli 1990), received AIA International Book Awards. Other books include *Portsmouth* (Studio Vista 1970), *Rockefeller Center: Architecture as Theater* (McGraw-Hill 1978).

Alan Balfour is Dean of the School of Architecture at Rensselaer and formerly Chairman of the Architectural Association in London. He was the year 2000 *Topaz Laureate*, the highest recognition given in North America to an academic in architecture.

Web address: **alanbalfour.com**

First published in Scotland in 2005
Published by Finlay Brown, Edinburgh
www.finlaybrown.com

Concept © Alan Balfour
Essays © The Authors
Photographs © Duccio Malagamba-fotografia de arquitectura S. L.
Miralles drawings © EMBT, Barcelona
Engravings of Edinburgh kindly supplied by Peter Stubbs
www.edinphoto.com

Designed by StudioLR, Edinburgh
www.StudioLR.com

Printed in Scotland

ISBN 0-9550016-0-9